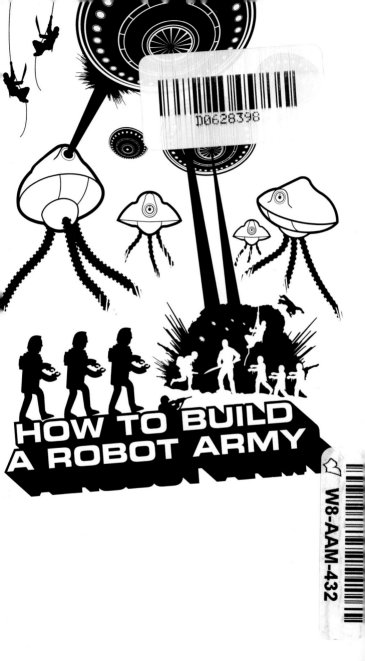

HOW TO BUILD
A ROBOT ARMY

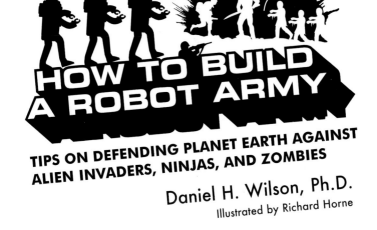

HOW TO BUILD A ROBOT ARMY

TIPS ON DEFENDING PLANET EARTH AGAINST ALIEN INVADERS, NINJAS, AND ZOMBIES

Daniel H. Wilson, Ph.D.

Illustrated by Richard Horne

BLOOMSBURY

BY THE SAME AUTHOR

HOW TO SURVIVE A ROBOT UPRISING
WHERE'S MY JETPACK?

Published by Bloomsbury USA, New York
Distributed to the trade by Holtzbrinck Publishers

Wilson, Daniel H. (Daniel Howard), 1978–   How to build a robot army:
tips on defending planet earth against alien invaders, ninjas, and zombies / Daniel H. Wilson.
p. cm.   ISBN 1-59691-281-2   ISBN-13 978-1-59691-281-6   1. Robots. 2. Robots—Humor. I. Title.
TJ211.W437 2008   629.8'92—dc22   2007060888

First U.S. Edition 2008

1 3 5 7 9 10 8 6 4 2

Designed and typeset by Richard Horne

Printed in China by South China Printing Co

www.howtobuildarobotarmy.com

FOR

EVAN ADDISON CARPENTER

FROM HIS GODFATHER

HOW TO BUILD A ROBOT ARMY

We all know that robots are bloodthirsty machines bent on wreaking havoc with humankind. But what about all the other menacing creatures that lurk in the shadows? Movie scripts and sci-fi books are bursting at the seams with threats to the human species. Other than robots, humankind is vulnerable to a host of unthinking enemies, including slimy aliens, slinking ninjas, and shambling zombies. Also, great white sharks. And unlike our robotic creations, these monsters cannot be remote-controlled, reprogrammed, or shut down. Vampires lust for our blood, werewolves stalk our children, and rogue asteroids hurtle toward our defenseless planet. To survive, we must look beyond the human-killing potential of robots and see them for what they really are: humankind's most powerful ally in the war against horror.

Consider this: During the coming apocalypse you may not be hit by a massive dose of gamma radiation and turned into an unstoppable mutant killing machine. Instead, in the future fray you will have to rely on your wits and on your limited human physique. In stark contrast to puny people, robots are highly specialized metallic superheroes capable of delivering diesel-powered scissor kicks and launching rocket fists at any time. A well-balanced combination of robots, humans, and slightly robotic humans constitutes our

best defense — no matter what monstrous foes those caffeine-addled Hollywood screenwriters concoct.

As the enemies of Earth multiply, brave scientists are developing new robot allies to shield our tender human bodies from insensate evil. Cold, hard reality is replacing what was once hot, throbbing science fiction. To that end, leading scientists in academia and industry contributed advice on every section of this book, whether it be mobilizing a team of metal-sheathed robots against zombies, staking out a werewolf-infested forest with auto-guns, or sending an autonomous underwater vehicle to hunt a man-killing great white shark.

In this book you will learn about every aspect of assembling and deploying a devastating robot horde. From weaponizing robotic household appliances to controlling swarms of metallic minions, you will receive step-by-step instructions for selecting appropriate robots, training them to fight, and commanding them in battle. Read this book, gather an army of mechanical mercenaries, and join the fight to protect the human way of life.

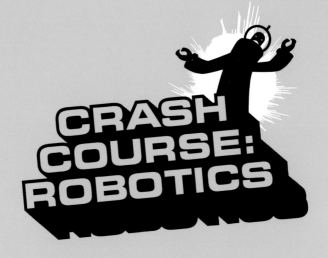

n 1956, the world saw its first modern robot, a steel arm dubbed "Unimate." The hardworking robot arm was rooted to one spot and was deaf, dumb, and blind. It also revolutionized heavy manufacturing, which now depends on millions of similar arms. Over fifty years later, one simple robot has evolved into thousands of robot varieties. Like in the animal kingdom, different species of robot function best in different environments. But unlike fuzzy animals, robots are also comfortable cruising in outer space, tunneling through radioactive waste, and traipsing through volcanic gases — and this is just the beginning . . .

The unifying framework behind every robot is the *sense-think-act* paradigm — the *closed-loop* process by which a robot senses the environment, thinks about what to do, and then acts in the physical world. The results of those actions are fed back into the "sensing step" for an ongoing trial-and-error strategy that is very similar to how we humans interact with the world. The loop requires *sensors* to gather information, *artificial intelligence* to decide on a course of action, and *end effectors* to interact with the environment. An artifact that does anything less is just a glorified remote-controlled car.

Robots are watching, listening, and more — using an

array of sensors to convert external stimuli into electrical signals. Familiar sensors include cameras, microphones, and touch-sensitive contact switches (often called "bumper bars"). Some versions of these sensors exceed human capabilities: Infrared cameras can see heat, hydrophones can hear under water, and ultrasonic sensors bounce sound off objects to feel them from afar. Intrinsic sensors like gyroscopes and accelerometers measure gravitational forces so that robots can balance. Other sensors are more foreign: Magnetometers detect the strength and alignment of magnetic fields, laser range-finders spray an area with invisible light and time the return trip of each ray, and chemical sensors smell trace amounts of pollutants from miles away. Robots see a world that is invisible to humankind.

After collecting information about the world, a robot has to figure out what it means and how to use it. Early research focused on using rule-based systems to solve highly structured problems with computational shortcuts and brute force computation. Such machines excel at playing games — you may recall that *Deep Fritz* beat the reigning human world chess champion Vladimir Kramnik in 2006 — but falter when faced with real-world complexity. That's why more recent research in the field of artificial intelligence takes a different approach: Humans teach the machines how to learn. Thus, instead of solving every problem outright, researchers create a smart machine that can learn from experience and work out the answers on its own. This approach is vital when humans cannot solve the problem in the first place, or when we have no idea what problems the robot will need to solve. Advanced research is focused largely on duplicating human abilities through speech recognition, computer vision, and learned control policies for moving the body. Modern robots are programmed to program themselves.

It is not enough to absorb information and think about it — if robots are going to roll with us, they have to act right. Robots use *actuators* to move their arms, legs, or razor-sharp tentacles. Generally, actuators are electromechanical motors that convert electricity to physical force. *Step motors* are used for precise movements, like adjusting wing flaps on a butterfly-sized aerial vehicle. Meanwhile, heavy-duty robots lift huge loads without overheating by using *hydraulic power* generated by pumping fluid or air through tubes. Very small robots may flex electrosensitive polymers called *artificial muscles*. The electrical energy usually comes from batteries, although larger robots — especially military bots — may be powered by internal combustion engines, much like a semi-trailer truck.

In short, robots are autonomous mechanical artifacts that come in a surprising number of sizes and shapes, use computers for brains, and move through the world with strong limbs of plastic and metal.

HOW TO BEFRIEND AN UNFAMILIAR ROBOT

Understanding human speech, gestures, and emotions are challenging problems for robots to solve — even more difficult than planning a war or karate-kicking. Human beings can seem strange and frightening to even the friendliest of robots, so follow these tips to befriend the robot citizens you meet on the street.

Use common sense

If a robot does not belong to you, is chained to a post, or is busy helping someone else, leave it alone. As a rule, *never* approach an unfamiliar robot in a militarized zone.

Don't interfere with an ongoing task

Robots can be single-minded while working. If a massive robot arm is busy stamp-welding tractor doors, don't walk over and ask it for directions to Tijuana.

Watch for signs of aggression

Look at the robot's LEDs. Are they glowing green . . . or red? Listen for the sound of weapons being cocked, Tasers being charged, or lawn mower blades spinning up to speed.

Approach slowly

A robot's range sensors may be inaccurate (making your pale, skinny legs hard to detect). Move slowly to give the robot a high certainty of your position, reducing the chance that it will falsely detect a collision and dart away into the night.

Smile broadly

Remove your hat, sunglasses, and/or fake moustache. With a clear view of your face (the world's most expressive emoticon), a robot can more easily deduce your friendly intentions.

Greet the robot simply

An inexpensive robot may have limited speech-recognition capabilities. Speak in a clear, loud voice and use short, simple words. Do *not* speak overly slowly — the robot is not trained to recognize slow-motion speech.

Extend your hand, palm out

Approach the robot slowly with your palm extended. The robot may sniff or lick your hand. Do not be alarmed; the robot is just getting to know you.

Always ask permission to pet someone else's robot

You wouldn't want some stranger putting their filthy hands all over *your* appliances.

When in doubt, obey human social rules

It is not okay to cut a robot off in line. It is not okay to shove a robot out of the elevator to make space. And it is not okay to steal a robot's Christmas sweater, push the robot down, and then say, "Get your own sweater, wimp." Remember: Robots are people, too.

We are entering the age of the robot. Unheard-of advances in computer vision, artificial intelligence, and locomotion have made robots more capable and numerous than ever before. If we are to cooperate with robots on bomb-scarred battlefields, we must first understand them. Prepare to learn everything you ever wanted to know about robots but were too terrified of disembowelment or decapitation (or both simultaneously) to ask.

Every robot can contribute to the survival of humans, whether it is a domestic appliance, an experimental prototype, or a battle-tested military drone. In a typical survival horror situation, a house full of domestic cleaning droids, furry robot toys, and a late-model car sitting in the garage may be the only thing standing between you and a rapidly breeding horde of slimy creatures. Learn to weaponize a vacuum robot, divert unwanted attention with a modified robo-kitty, or transform your late-model car into a subservient unmanned ground vehicle. You never know when you might need to toss homemade pipe bombs through the sunroof while your trusty vehicle nimbly dodges laser beams.

Robot appliances and toys are mass-produced, but many other robots are one-of-a-kind. The robotic prototypes that live in universities are unique, rare, and buggy, but solve problems that tried-and-true robots

cannot. Experimental robots may be built from strange, musclelike materials, on incredibly small scales, or to do outrageous things, like landing on an asteroid or performing a double backflip. In cases of national emergency, desperate human governments (or what is left of them) may draw upon these extraordinary prototypes to solve extraordinary problems.

Student-built bots shuffle through university hallways, but the world's battle zones are reserved for military bots. Treaded, lawn mower–sized robots routinely dismantle improvised explosive devices with their bare hands and are commonly blown to pieces. In the sky, hovering drones ceaselessly circle the desolate landscape while bird-sized micro air vehicles flit through the city streets below. There may be days, hours, or milliseconds between now and a future in which hip underground gangs of street-racing vampires flood our streets. In this chapter, we will learn how to utilize every available robot to protect our precious planet.

ROBOTS IN THE HOME

When the time comes, the first line of robo-defense will emerge directly from our homes. As more and more robots hit store shelves, the American populace is slowly but surely building a massive standing army of robotic appliances.

What used to be simple appliances like vacuums, mops, and lawn mowers are steadily being replaced by affordable robot lackeys; children's toys can walk, talk, and giggle maniacally (thank you, Tickle Me Elmo); and late-model automobiles roll off the assembly line with an array of built-in robotic abilities: Adaptive cruise control uses the gas pedal, traction control hits the brakes, and *drive-by-wire* systems can even steer. Soon, all your housework and errands may be done by robots at the push of a button. (Except for the robot that pushes the button, to whom you shout, "Push it, robot!")

In this section, we will discover how to arm the robots in our homes for battle. Although not built to fight, these robots are efficient and reliable enough to have trickled down from a few research laboratories to millions of homes nationwide. Their robotic abilities may have been honed for cleaning floors, entertaining children, and sitting in traffic, but with the right knowledge and proper preparation even the most innocuous robot can be transformed into a powerful ally in the struggle against mummies.

DOMESTIC BOTS

Robotic appliances are not as simple as they seem; they have to reliably re-create the abilities of human beings for complicated cleaning tasks and they have to do it for a few hundred bucks. What looks like a dull-witted hunk of junk may actually be an elegant, stripped-down solution to a complicated engineering problem. Never fear: The limited intellect and physical prowess of housebound robots can be put to good use in the future Armageddon.

Domestic droids are commonly designed to vacuum, mop, or mow. As single-purpose machines, these robots use a minimal number of sensors and simple artificial intelligence (AI) to accomplish a single task. Instead of expensive cameras and laser range-finders, these robots have bumper bars and infrared (IR) signal receivers — like on a TV remote. Already in millions of homes, the iRobot Roomba is a disc-shaped piece of plastic about the diameter of a dinner plate and three inches tall — short enough to scoot under the couch. The Roomba vacuums semi-randomly, bouncing between chair legs and tracing its way around walls like a toddler on skates. Its bigger brother, the Dirt Dog, can suck up nuts and bolts off the garage floor without choking. In the kitchen, the iRobot Scooba rides a few millimeters off the floor and uses a brush-and-squeegee system to clean tile and hardwood. Mowing robots, such as the RoboMower from Friendly Robotics, roam the yard mulching grass with blades whirring at 5,800 rpm and using sonar range-finders to avoid sunbathers and family pets.

Robotic appliances are so simpleminded that it is often up to their human owners to babysit them. The real world is an *unstructured environment* — a place where anything can happen — and no special exceptions are made for robots. On the other hand, *structured environments* may have specially monitored temperatures, lighting conditions, noise levels, and/or visual markers. For example, robo-mowers are kept from roaming the streets by sensing perimeter wires painstakingly buried by the human owner. Although the Roomba can vacuum, it can't identify shoelaces (its only eyes are a bumper bar and infrared proximity sensors). Instead, vacuuming robots rely on their human keepers to create a structured environment by picking up clutter, cordoning off the area to be vacuumed with infrared beam generators, and providing an occasional rescue and arm-cradle airlift back to the charging station. Luckily for robots, the average home is already a moderately structured place equipped with flat floors, good lighting, and insulation from the weather. Even so, humans who want to live in a fully automatized robot ecosystem should expect to make a few changes; for example, prototype dishwashing droids like the ARMAR humanoid from the University of Karlsruhe require brightly colored plastic dishes.

In an emergency, weaponizing a small household robot can be a lifesaving opportunity — or an opportunity for disaster. In TV shows like *Robot Wars* and *BattleBots*, participants convert ordinary appliances into radio-controlled robots armed with spikes, whirling lawn mower blades, and pneumatic hammers. During the first season of *Robot Wars*, a two-hundred-pound spike-covered robot went haywire and impaled a spectator through the heel. Another unwary participant had his teeth smashed out by a suddenly activated hammer. Consider yourself warned: It's all fun and games until Roomba disembowels you and refuses to clean up the mess.

HOW TO WEAPONIZE A ROBOTIC VACUUM

Pop culture threats are hard to predict. So, when a teenaged gang of vampires with bleached hair and leather jackets hovers outside your windows waiting to suck your blood, you may have to follow these steps and pull a MacGyver on the simple robo-vacuum obliviously cleaning your carpet. Your robot sidekick probably cost a few hundred dollars — consider it a down payment on the rest of your life.

Brainwash the robot

Most robots have a hidden port that allows a personal computer to interface with the "brain." Follow instructions from the manufacturer and brainwash (or *mod*) the robot's behavior: Disable unwanted sensors, turn off the vacuum pump, and erase the robot's preprogrammed tendency to clean rather than fight aliens.

Let domestic bots fight on their own turf

The average domestic robot is not so much a technological terror as it is an overcooked appliance. Assume a specialized robot will fail to work outside its designated area. Robo-vacuums can handle hardwood floors and thin carpet — rug fringes are a tricky wild card.

Upgrade the robot to take it off-road

A bumper bar will trigger off uneven ground, keeping your robot trapped in the house. Use a pair of pliers to

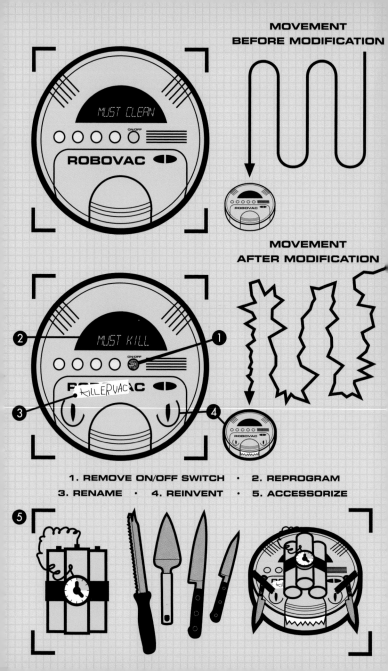

cut away the plastic on the bottom of the front bumper bar or remove it entirely to take the fight outside of your living room.

Send commands via remote control

An IR remote control requires line of sight to the robot (bouncing the signal off a wall is possible, but not consistent), so find a good hiding spot before guiding your robot conscript into the fray.

Put a brick on the gas pedal

To force a vacuum forward, fold a matchbook and place it over the Forward button of the remote control. Wrap duct tape around the remote so that the button is constantly pressed. Now tape the remote to the top of the robot. Put it on the sidewalk and let it go.

Structure the environment — your way

Many robot vacuum cleaners come with IR beam generators that create artificial, invisible boundaries. Place two of these side by side to create a "corridor." The robot will bounce between the two "walls" and go where you aim it — for instance, into the gaping maw of an alien beast.

Weaponize it

Convert your harmless robo-cleaner into a mechanized soldier fighting for the forces of awesomeness. Here are a few approaches:

→ *Add passive weapons.* Duct tape a pair of scissors (or a steak knife) to the top. Consider aiming the knife straight up, in case an enemy steps on your low-profile bot.

→ *Cause a distraction.* Tape a flashlight or a beeping smoke alarm to the top of the robot and send it out into the night. The vacuum itself generates about 80 decibels of noise — not quite as loud as a blender, but enough to get the attention of a stalking werewolf.

→ *Create a roving land mine.* Place a can of gas on top of the robot, send it trundling away, and then shoot the can from a distance. Alternately, strap a stick of dynamite on top and wire the detonator to the bumper bar. The little guy will blow when he hits his first obstacle.

→ *Be safe: Include an emergency stop.* A robot gone *loco* will only help the foes of humanity. Include a physically accessible emergency stop button (or removable link). Resist the urge to place the "e-stop" in a cute location, such as the nose. While this may be aesthetically pleasing, it could prove fatal in an actual emergency.

ROBOT PETS

Robots have an unjust reputation as cold, emotionless metal beings. An alternative was presented in the 2001 movie *Artificial Intelligence: A.I.*, in which a cuddly robotic teddy bear (aptly named Teddy) kept a little boy safe while acting as a super playmate. Similarly, a slew of real-life robot companions are set to challenge robot stereotypes. In fact, cuddly robot pets of the future will look and act so naturally that the adjective "robotic" may soon become an anachronism.

Box-loads of mewling kittens are ready and waiting next to the highway, but modern kids want to cuddle dinosaurs and cartoons. The Ugobe company offers Pleo, an infant Camarasaurus (a paleontologist consulted on the design) with a constantly evolving personality. Pleo uses three-dozen touch, sound, light, and tilt sensors to understand the world, and fourteen motors to walk, rear up on two feet, and even limp when "hurt." Meanwhile, the fuzzy red Tickle Me Elmo eXtreme (TMX) from Tyco can roll on the floor laughing, pound its fists on the ground, and beg for the tickler to just "please stop it." The demonically giggling robot — not unlike Chucky from the movies — is sure to terrorize parents for years to come.

Robot toys are ready to serve as entertainers, but other robot pets are designed to accompany children into the perilous world, keeping them safe. Researchers at the Massachusetts Institute of Technology (MIT) designed a real-life version of Teddy; "Huggable" the robot bear cannot walk, but it can move its neck, shoulders, and face. It senses the world with camera-eyes, microphone-ears, and a sensitive skin-layer that detects electrical field, temperature, and force. Via an embedded computer, Huggable can transmit this data across a wireless network back to caregivers, parents, or other narcs. If a kid can't trust his teddy bear, who's left to trust?

Kids are not the only ones who deserve toys. At the Intelligent Systems Research Institute in Japan, a baby robot seal named Paro uses its fuzzy white pelt and big, wide eyes to manipulate the emotions of the elderly. Paro looks like a cute but unfamiliar baby harp seal so that people will have no preconceptions about how it should act. In therapy, interacting with the fuzzy bot has proven to lower stress levels, reduce heart and respiratory rate, and increase the self-reported levels of happiness of participants. Physicians also benefit because Paro collects and reports health data. Researchers already knew that animal companionship helps people; surprisingly, robotic companionship also delivers positive psychological (e.g., relaxation), physiological (e.g., lower blood pressure), and social effects (e.g., incessant giggling).

HOW TO USE A PET ROBOT TO TERRORIZE YOUR ENEMIES

When it comes to intimidation, nothing complements your cold, psychopathic demeanor like a furry, harmless-looking pet. Whether you are representing the planet in negotiations with alien overlords or trying to squeeze information from a recalcitrant pirate, your child's mechanical pet can be a useful tool for instilling terror.

Keep it hypoallergenic

Animal fur is full of dander that can cause nasty allergies. Lovable robots, however, come equipped with hypoallergenic fur that releases no allergens and will not cause you to sneeze in the middle of a rambling monologue.

Go for the exotic

There is no limit to the size and shape of your robo-companion. Off-the-shelf pets come as conventional animals, dinosaurs, or humanoids. Customized pet robots could be something unique (a miniature elephant), mythical (a three-headed dog), or patriotic (a mini–Statue of Liberty).

Agree on a secret language

High-dollar robot pets can check the weather, read emails, and understand speech. Work out a series of kneads, flipper pats, or code grunts that secretly enact

preprogrammed sequences. When you stand unarmed before your arch-nemesis, just gently meow like an alley cat to spring open that trap door.

Incorporate biometrics

Any pet — real or robot — better love its owner more than anybody else. Install a fingerprint reader, iris scanner, or face-recognition system so your pet will recognize you (and hiss and swipe at anybody else). After all, isn't that what having a pet is all about?

Initiate kill-mode

Pet robots are harmless and lovable — until the owner welds on a set of metal claws and teaches the robot a cute (and deadly) wiggle dance. For a surprise attack, "accidentally" drop your cuddle-bot on the floor and watch as it launches itself into the air and latches onto the face of your unsuspecting enemy.

Install a self-destruct sequence

You may love your pet, but don't forget that it's only a robot. Wedge a hunk of plastic explosive into your little friend so that someday it may save your life.

Consider something cut-rate

A Tamagotchi is a keychain-sized pet that requires constant feeding and supervision or else it will die painfully and noisily. Fun!

UNMANNED
GROUND VEHICLES

A modern robot car is not so different from the hunk of metal sitting in your driveway. Taking a cue from *Knight Rider*, researchers have found that the most cost-effective and reliable approach to building an unmanned ground vehicle (UGV) is to hack into the computer of a black 1982 Pontiac Trans-Am — or better yet, a 2005 Volkswagen Touareg.

The Defense Advanced Research Projects Agency (DARPA) was founded in 1958 and tasked with maintaining the technological superiority of the US military. To push the development of driverless cars, DARPA sponsors a semi-annual "Grand Challenge" in which UGVs race each other for fun and profit. During the 2005 DARPA Grand Challenge, the winning team (from Stanford) transformed a Volkswagen Touareg into the all-powerful "Stanley." The unassuming UGV autonomously tore across 132 miles of desert in just under seven hours — through tunnels, between gates, and around other UGVs — clinching the win with an average speed of 19.1 mph. A key lesson: Mechanical control was achieved by merely hacking into the electronic control unit (ECU). The ECU is the "brain" of the car, containing a separate module (called a *bus*) for each part of the car, such as the safety bus for airbags and antilock brakes, a comfort bus for air-conditioning and seat position, and a control bus for gas, brake, and gear shifter. Direct access to a central ECU now makes robot control more reliable and precise than ever.

A robot car needs eyes and ears. Many internal sensors are already integrated into the car, including an odometer, a gas gauge, and an inertial measurement unit (IMU). External sensors are usually added to a roof rack: light detection and ranging (LIDAR), radar systems, and cameras.

Each sensor fills in a different part of the picture. Laser range-finders spot obstacles accurately but have range limits of around one hundred feet. (Using LIDAR alone limits top speed to 25 mph — like driving at night with weak headlights.) High-powered radar extends this range; unfortunately, the signal picks up metallic objects (like cars) and tends to pass right through organic entities (like your grandpa). Cameras step in to fill the gap, detecting distant organic objects better than radar or laser, but with much lower accuracy and more vulnerability to dust and vibration. With all three sensors working together, the safe top speed of a UGV exceeds 40 mph.

Even with control and access to extra sensors, the car still needs to learn how to drive. Luckily, its smarts are often freely available for download from universities. It works like this: A *mapper* creates a three-dimensional map based on the sensor information. Each square of the map is marked as "safe," "unsafe," or "unknown." Next, a *path planner* determines the best route from point A to point B that stays on the safe squares. As it drives, the car performs *pose estimation* to figure out where it's located, what direction it's oriented, and how fast it's moving.

The next challenge for UGVs is to leave the desert and move into the cities. In the 2007 DARPA Urban Challenge about ninety UGVs will be unleashed on a peaceful mock city abandoned by humans but teeming with drone traffic. Unlike the desert racers of the 2005 DARPA Grand Challenge, these driverless cars must avoid obstacles and obey traffic signals while merging, passing, and parking in order to net the two-million-dollar grand prize (the runner-up gets a paltry million). After this competition, expect even better robot brains and instruction guides to be made available by the competing teams.

HOW TO CONVERT YOUR CAR INTO AN UNMANNED GROUND VEHICLE

An unmanned ground vehicle doesn't need you or anybody else. Put the "auto" in automobile and you will be free to man the Uzi while your trusty robot car dodges skittering monsters and runs down squishy alien beings.

Choose a late-model car

Cars produced after about the mid-1990s are easier to hack because the engine, gas, and brakes are managed by an electronic control unit. If electronic access is not possible, be aware that most modern cars use low-level artificial intelligence algorithms that monitor engine conditions to tailor the amount of gas and brake to apply — so, pushing the gas pedal the same way twice can have varying results.

Jury-rig mechanical parts

If computerized steering control is unavailable, slap a motorcycle chain around sprockets placed on the steering wheel and rotate it with a DC motor. A gear shifter can be moved by a linear actuator bolted onto the shifting stick.

Give the UGV eyes and ears

Use the electronic control unit to access existing sensors, such as the speedometer. Mount extra sensors to a roof rack, including a light detection and ranging unit, a high-powered radar system, and binocular cameras with depth perception.

Maintain your sensors

In a study of twenty-four UGVs at the University of South Florida, the camera was found to be by far the most failed sensor, usually due to occlusion and incorrect lighting. Wipe dirt and mud off the sensors, keep the vehicle headlights on bright, and secure the roof rack tightly to minimize vibration.

Use GPS, but do not rely on it

The global positioning system can provide three-dimensional coordinates, but measurements are often noisy or missing due to spotty satellite coverage and interference from buildings and trees. For what it's worth, the best GPS receivers on the market are used by farmers to plow their fields into perfectly straight rows.

Insert the computer brain — it's alive!

A UGV does not need a supercomputer. Use one personal computer to process sensor information and another to make decisions and control the car. Open-source software for controlling the car is available on the Internet — designing the car's sensitive but spunky personality is up to you.

Stick to the highway

The open road requires fewer sensors than an urban environment because more time is spent looking straight ahead than monitoring the situation all around. Trust a hastily constructed UGV to work better on the highway than in a complicated urban environment.

Put in a sweet T-top

A sleek T-top can transform a regular car into a "glamour hammer."

Insurance may be a problem

A street-legal car must have a human driver, so make sure that your UGV has a space for a person to take temporary control. If the car has a wreck while you are asleep in the back seat, the authorities probably will not know who to blame — as of yet, there is no legal precedent.

Alternately, buy a remote-controlled drone

Drone SUVs for the military are built by Autonomous Solutions Inc., in Utah. Ask for the "Proving Grounds Automation Package," drop off the family car, and pick up your new robo-vehicle a few weeks later. With the "barebones" package (around $100,000) your talented car can be remote-controlled or programmed to run routes without a driver.

Get out there and fight some crime!

The world is depending on you and your talking robot car to protect them from villains with bad hair and tight blue jeans.

HELLO
MY NAME IS
FXB-902

ROBOTS IN THE LABORATORY

Earth's most advanced robots reside in university and industry laboratories: nano-robots that can enter your body through a single pore of your skin, shape-shifting robots that would tear a T-1000 Terminator to shreds, and cyborg insects that could give Stephen King the willies. Thus, it is to the university robots (and their keepers) that we must turn in the event of a worldwide catastrophe, such as a rapidly spreading zombie infestation.

University research is the engine that drives the field of robotics forward. It works like this: A professor gathers a team of bright-eyed graduate students and applies for a grant. With the money, the professor buys equipment and pays graduate students to devote years of their young lives to designing and building robots. Papers are written. Videos are made of the robot in action (and then sped up so as not to be boring). Ultimately, the rest of the scientific community scours the robot for flaws and corrections are made. In academia, only the strongest robots survive.

In this section, we learn to draw on the amazing capabilities of an elite class of experimental robots. Laboratory robots are delicate, but they possess unique powers largely unknown to the rest of the world. These robots are described in technical papers and patent applications instead of in the Sharper Image catalog. Nevertheless, knowing what capabilities exist on the cutting edge of science will be crucial to human survival as we hurtle into the twenty-first century.

MICRO-ROBOTS

A squirming mass of micro-robots are infiltrating the human body. The conventional locomotion techniques used by larger robots fail on the microscale needed to move through veins and intestines, so innovative scientists are taking inspiration from a biological world teeming with microscopic bugs and parasites.

The scenic gateways to your internal organs are located where food goes in and where it comes out. Like worms and leeches, robots who want to locomote down the back of your throat or up your colon must use *undulatory* motion. Two approaches work: a side-to-side, snakelike wiggle (which allows for swimming, should things get watery) or an earthwormlike scrunching motion in which the body alternately shrinks and elongates (*peristaltic* locomotion). Both techniques have been demonstrated in nasal and colon cavities by tiny robotic prototypes. Dutch researchers from the Delft University of Technology developed "wormbots," intestinal travelers able to wriggle through the lower intestine without damaging the sensitive terrain.

Smaller-scale surgical robots are somehow less gross. Researchers at the NanoRobotics Laboratory at Carnegie Mellon University (CMU) are developing micro-robots to swim through the syrupy, viscous fluid inside the human renal system. Boat propellers flounder on such a small scale, so the millimeter-sized CMU micro-robots copy the propulsion techniques of bacteria and spermatozoa, which use taillike *flagella* and *cilia* to swim. These robots copy nature by spinning a synthetic helical tail, moving much like a corkscrew through a wine cork. The tiny bot moves at about six feet per hour — ten times faster than regular *E. coli* bacteria.

As fast as robo-bacteria move, though, the nano-manipulation techniques necessary to build them are prohibitively expensive. Sticking out your thumb and hitching a ride from hardworking natural bacteria, however, is free. The same CMU researchers have literally harnessed the power of bacteria by building *hybrid micro-robots*. Here is how it's done: A colony of the fastest nonpathogenic species of bacteria is purchased from a genetic bank. Back at the lab, a tiny robot (with no propulsion system) is coated with a special chemical and dipped into "microbe city" for about five minutes. During this time, anywhere from ten to one hundred bacteria may decide to bond with the robot. Once the bacteria are hitched up, a set of onboard chemicals excite them into wiggling frantically or lull them into sitting still. The robot buggy and its microbe steeds are ready to wriggle into your body to keep you in prime physical condition, but it will be a one-way journey — unfed, the bacteria will starve to death in two to three hours and then quickly biodegrade.

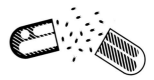

 UP TO FOUR MILLION MICRO-ROBOTS PER DOSE FOR BODY RECONFIGURATION

HOW TO SUPERCHARGE YOUR BODY WITH MICRO-ROBOTS

Robots are shrinking in size and growing inside you — and that's not a bad thing. Millimeter-sized robots can swim throughout your body, sensing and reporting internal conditions and even knocking out nasty medical problems, like kidney stones. Someday, a proper diet of robotic antibodies may render you impervious to germ warfare.

Use human-friendly materials

Materials that are safe inside the human body are called *biocompatible.* Materials made from surgical stainless steel (e.g., medical instruments) and silicone (e.g., contact lenses) are the most common and safe to incorporate into your body. Your local tattoo and piercing shop should have a supply of biocompatible metals and plastics such as titanium and Teflon on hand, especially if they offer subdermal implants.

Sterilize before you internalize

For a hybrid nano-robot, just make sure that the bacterial propulsion you use is non-disease-causing. Synthetically propelled micro-robots, however, should be sterilized to remove bacteria, fungi, and viruses. Heat sterilization is common — simply use a lighter to heat the metal until it glows. (Hospitals use an *autoclave* that steams at 121° Celsius for fifteen minutes.) Alternately, dunk the micro-robot in bleach for twenty minutes.

TO BE TAKEN INTERNALLY

MAGNIFIED x1000 TIMES
EACH PILL CONTAINS UP TO
FOUR MILLION NANOBOTS.
THE EASY WAY TO REBUILD,
REPAIR AND REINVIGORATE
YOUR OLD AND TIRED BODY.

Take the urethra highway

From an engineering perspective, the human renal system is one of the simplest environments in which a micro-robot can locomote within the body. Keep this in mind when you try to plan the fastest route — "Google BodyMaps" never pays attention.

Swallow a camera-bot

Used for endoscopy, vitamin-pill-sized robots can cruise down your throat and snap photos during the picturesque journey through your guts. Don't worry, you will "pass" the robot naturally within twenty-four to seventy-two hours. Note: Think twice before reusing this robot.

Sit on a bug-bot

There is a party in your pants and only the robots are invited. Reverse versions of swallowable camera-bots come with tiny legs. Polymer pads on the leg tips adhere to intestinal walls to allow some limited locomotion in your slippery lower intestine.

Ensure graceful degradation

Make sure that the robot inside you will be expelled naturally and not become lodged in your heart. The intestinal tract and renal system are considered safe, but your veins can carry robots to unwanted places.

Consider keyhole surgery

In an emergency, save the robot some travel time and consider *keyhole surgery*, in which doctors poke a tiny hole in your body and insert a tethered robot on the end of a steel arm. Better yet, let a robot cut the entry hole — robotic incisions are cleaner than human ones and heal faster.

HUMANOID ROBOTS

When humans inevitably charge into battle together with humanoid robots, it will not be alongside the sneering metallic skeletons that pervaded the *Terminator* trilogy. Humanoid robots are built primarily for use by ordinary people, not soldiers. When horror strikes, we will be more likely to draft our diminutive, cute androids as conscripts. Saving humanity calls for more than smearing warpaint on your butler's face and shoving it into the fight — you have got to learn all about humanoid robots.

Humanoid robots are general-purpose robots that look much like people, replete with head, torso, arms, and legs. The "total package" humanoid can walk like a person and also use its hands to dexterously manipulate objects in the world. Curiously, the most advanced humanoids originate from car companies. Under secret development by Honda since the 1980s, the constantly evolving ASIMO can now run at 3.7 mph, climb stairs reliably, and push a drink cart. The size of a twelve-year-old kid, ASIMO is just tall enough to see over countertops and to reach up and hold your hand. Although human-controlled ASIMO units perform demonstrations all over the world, only one lonely, autonomous ASIMO exists; he lives in a basement laboratory at Carnegie Mellon University. Honda has a stiff competitor in the Partner Robot division of Toyota. For the 2005 World Expo in Japan, Toyota manufactured one hundred humanoid robots that marched together in a parade and played real instruments, using air compressors to blow into horns and fingers to manipulate valves and slides.

Corporate humanoids are usually developed in total secrecy, but a long-lost cousin of ASIMO is open-source and available for purchase, offering university researchers the chance to develop the brains behind the humanoid brawn. The HRP-3P is an early Honda ASIMO model that was purchased and built upon by Kawada Industries. The water- and dustproof humanoid was made for walking outdoors on roads, sidewalks, and grass. (It has even walked on Teflon, which is about as slick as ice.) The 145-pound HRP-3P stands five feet three inches tall and uses binocular and trinocular vision to walk for about two hours on one battery charge. Incidentally, the last "P" stands for "prototype." The upcoming HRP-3 will be a leap forward — a female humanoid with sleek plastic curves reminiscent of Maria, the sexy fembot from the movie *Metropolis*.

Unlike other humanoid robots, androids are less about function and more about form. Aside from being unable to walk, the most advanced mechanical simulacrums are initially indistinguishable from humans. At the Japanese ATR Intelligent Robotics and Communication Laboratory, an angry-looking android was created in the image of its maker, Dr. Hiroshi Ishiguro. Geminoid HI-1 not only looks like a fully clothed person, but it also re-creates human *micromovements* by blinking, fidgeting, and pretending to breathe. Meanwhile, female androids are universally sexy. The Actroid DER2 robot from the Kokoro-Dreams company wears a tight Hello Kitty sweater and glossy pink lipstick. The fembot uses pneumatic actuators to cheerfully gesture while delivering choreographed talks and is available to rent for a few thousand dollars a day. And for those who dream of cold, passionless robot sex, there's a German aircraft mechanic who will add internal heaters, actuated hips, and a mechanical beating heart to silicone-skinned (and usually inert) Love Dolls. (You'll have to look him up for yourself, sicko.)

Humanoid robots re-create human mobility and manipulation, but look like plastic space cadets. On the other hand, androids pull off natural human communication with voice, gesture, and even emotion, but the illusion is lost without full mobility. Bridging this gap to create the ultimate humanoid android has caught the interest of universities and industry, and become a badge of pride for entire nations. In fact, rumor has it that a Chinese-built humanoid robot will light the torch at the 2008 Beijing Olympics.

HOW TO KEEP A SEXY FEMBOT FIT FOR BATTLE

You never plan on living with a female android — it just sort of happens. At first it seems like the ultimate male fantasy: to live with a beautiful woman who is programmed to obey. It soon becomes obvious, however, that a fembot is stronger, smarter, and sexier than any male counterpart. Don't despair: Her superiority makes the fembot perfectly suited to act as your first line of defense when your neighborhood becomes a battle zone.

Don't get attached

It is only natural for humans to form a deep social attachment with a girl-shaped hunk of plastic. Resist this urge and concentrate on objectifying the woman-bot. In a life-or-death situation you cannot hesitate to hand your fembot a cutlass and send her into battle against foulmouthed, male-chauvinist pirates.

Consider a nonhuman form factor

Are you turned on by the girl next door, or by a ten-foot-tall tentacled hentai monster? Interesting physical anomalies can make your fembot sexier and deadlier; so don't be afraid to add extra arms, squishy tentacles, or eggbeaters for hands.

Be wary if she forgets your birthday

If she forgot your birthday, your eye color, or the number of bullets left in the clip, it was intentional.

Score points

A less-than-happy fembot may balk at throwing herself into danger on your account. If unsure of her loyalties, casually check the fembot's high-score list for your initials.

Check out her past — look up her VIN

You don't want to enter battle only to find your fembot has a painted fiberglass hull and not the titanium she promised. And you definitely don't want to find out how many modifications your fembot has had by looking into the hideously ugly face of your first robot child. Play it safe and call the Department of Motor Vehicles to look up her vehicle identification number.

Don't expect the human touch

Robots can be rough on the battlefield and in the bedroom, so protect yourself: Wear a Kevlar vest, lower-back support, and an antistatic bracelet tied to a metal bedpost.

ROBOT BUGS

Bugs are everywhere. Millions of species of insects (many of which are still unidentified) have evolved to live in nearly every environment on the globe. As inferior human beings, we can only hope to copy our diminutive neighbors and incorporate their physical abilities and instinctive behaviors into the most powerful robots that ever crawled, wriggled, or hopped across the planet.

Waterstrider

Researchers at the CMU NanoRobotics Laboratory have blown a tiny phenomenon up to size — the waterstrider bug. About as big as a nickel, these insects use a wide stance and water-repellent legs to skate across the surface of water. The principle was incorporated into STRIDE (Surface Tension Robot Insect Dynamic Explorer), a self-contained waterstrider robot the size of a cat. The spindly robot has twelve legs and weighs only a quarter of an ounce with all electronics, sensors, and a battery.

STRIDE floats because its springy wire feet push off the surface tension of the water, dimpling but not piercing the surface. The legs are positioned at optimal angles to spread the load broadly. In addition, each "foot" is coated with spray-on Teflon, which further repels water molecules. Two extra feet act as paddles to push the floating platform over as little as an eighth of an inch of water. The prototype robot has only been tested on smooth water — ripples would probably topple it. However, there is no theoretical limit to scale: Researchers predict that by increasing the surface area of the feet with mesh and increasing the water repellency with nanoscale fibers, a waterstriding robot could help reduce drag on a platform the size of a cargo ship.

Cyborg Insects

Why create robotic versions of insects when we can team up with the real thing? Regular insects can be remotely controlled or even crammed into the cockpit of larger robots to create cyborg bugs. It is no joke — a DARPA proposal calls for development of an insect-cyborg that can find a target around a hundred yards away, get within fifteen feet, and then transmit data from onboard sensors. Researchers believe that by implanting a micro-electromechanical system (MEMS) at the pupa stage, insects will integrate the devices seamlessly into their bodies — like a tree growing through a fence. At Tokyo University, researchers have already surgically implanted hardy American cockroaches with tiny radio-controlled "backpacks" that use electrodes wired into the antennae to trick (i.e., viciously shock) the insect into turning or moving forward or backward.

In another score for humankind's quest for cyborg insect armies, a giant Madagascan hissing cockroach has been trained to drive a trash-can-sized robot. A master's student at the University of California, Irvine, placed a three-inch-long roach atop a trackball that spins as the roach runs. Based on the direction of the spin, motors then move the wheeled robot around the room. Don't worry about the poor filthy roach — it is held in place by a small piece of Velcro harmlessly glued to its fingernail-like carapace.

Spiders

Don't laugh, but NASA believes that the future of extravehicular robotics (EVR) may depend on a race of giant, space-faring robot spiders. As space science platforms (e.g., satellites and solar panels) have grown in size, they have become too large and flimsy to launch in one piece. That's why the field of EVR focuses on coming up with gentle methods of locomotion and manipulation for constructing and maintaining orbiting structures. Spiders may be ferocious predators, but they walk with a soft touch. In outer space, weight does not matter but mass does — a nimble, spiderlike gait could be just the ticket.

With this in mind, NASA developed an arachnid robot to stalk around the outside of a fragile spaceship. The Spidernaut prototype is an eight-legged, six-hundred-pound golden monstrosity the size of a small car. The robot uses the multipoint stance of an arachnid, in which up to seven legs touch while it walks, distributing force evenly and imparting minimal torque (which could spin the spacecraft the robot is walking on). With such a gait, the spidery system could transport large payloads throughout a space construction site without pushing the structure out of its orbit.

Ants

We humans may not be as successful as we think. There is another worldwide society, made up of over ten thousand species of small, six-legged arthropods, that outnumbers us a million to one. Ants exist in extremely complex societies and cooperate to dominate every environmental niche they invade. Roboticists have found value in studying not only the physical structure of ants but also the highly effective social fabric that ties ant colonies together.

Ants use highly specific sensors that directly report important conditions: location, danger, or the presence of food. The inner workings of these sensors are important to roboticists because they naturally filter irrelevant information and reduce computational complexity. Scientists at the University of Ülm in Germany predicted that ants use an internal "pedometer" to count their steps and figure out their location. The researchers allowed regular Saharan desert ants to learn the distance between a nest and a food source. For half the ants they amputated a millimeter of leg and for the other half they attached one-millimeter "stilts." On the way back to the nest, ants with shorter legs stopped early and ants with longer legs went too far. An altered stride length confused the ants, proving that they had counted their steps.

Meanwhile, many researchers copy ant *swarm* behavior to help teams of micro-robots communicate and coordinate on tasks ranging from searching earthquake rubble for survivors to performing endoscopic surgery. Researchers at MIT developed a hundred-strong swarm of cubic-inch-sized Swarmbots that exhibited cooperative foraging behavior similar to real ants. The small form factor is important — materials grow relatively stronger as they shrink in size, because as mass shrinks, the impact of force lessens.

HOW TO DEPLOY SPYING ROBOT BUGS

Insects are small, agile, and chock-full of delicate sensory equipment. With a little help from robots, people can harness the mighty power of bug-kind and send cyborg bugs, robotic versions of bugs, and bugs that "drive" robot vehicles to infest our enemies with tiny spying eyes. Remember: If you need information, plant a bug.

Send them out in swarms

For large groups of simple robots, a swarm configuration will increase reliability and make your robo-bugs look more like the real thing. Program them to reenact honed ant behaviors such as foraging and attacking.

Choose lightweight sensors

A cockroach can lift twenty times its own weight, but it weighs less than a tenth of an ounce. A miniature microphone or camera is probably the limit for a natural insect.

Take advantage of insect sensors

Many insects are incredibly sensitive to useful stimuli — like the chemical signature left by a cache of explosives. Researchers at the University of Georgia developed the "Wasp Hound" by placing a trained wasp (*Microplitis croceipes*) into a box that relays when the wasp detects certain chemicals.

Stay close

The tiny radio transmitters that fit on insects or insect-sized robots have a short range. Alternately, use a distributed strategy and have the robots pass information back along a trail of properly stationed robot spies.

Create a distraction

Lobbing grenades at the hull of a spaceship may distract the occupants while your robo-ants work their way through cracks. Any rubble gives a tiny bot more hiding places.

Put bugs inside robots

Placing a bug inside a robot takes advantage of the instinctual behavior that comes with the insect's natural neural net. Surround a cockroach cockpit with lights that grow brighter as obstacles approach to make the darkness-loving bug less likely to crash its mini-*Mobile Suit Gundam*.

Attack on all fronts

Plague your enemy with robots and insects suited for the ground, sea, and air. While they swat robo-roaches, enemies might not notice that ant watching from the ceiling with beady metal eyes.

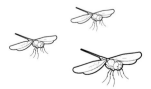

SHAPE-CHANGING ROBOTS

Like mighty Voltron (defender of the universe), the best robots of all are built out of . . . more robots. Shape-changers, called *modular robots*, are a conglomeration of autonomous robots (called *modules*) that can wriggle around and lock into arbitrary configurations: humanoid, arachnid, or robot grizzly bear. *Self-reconfigurable* robots can change shape on their own, while simpler transforming robots may require the help of a twelve-year-old. Clearly, these "transformers" are more than meets the eye.

They may not lie awake at night wondering about it, but modular robots are either homo or hetero: *Homogenous* robots are built from identical, interchangeable modules, and *heterogeneous* robots are a mix of generic and special-purpose modules. Homogenous modules are easy to replace, but without single-purpose modules, simple tasks may become unnecessarily complex. For example, instead of just using well-placed wheels, a homogenous robot must transform itself into a giant rolling loop. Heterogeneous robots are more generally used in practice, where they have proven capable of self-repair, self-assembly, and locomotion over many types of terrain.

Modular robots can be divided into three classes: *chain*, *lattice*, and *hybrid*. Chain-type robots connect into long, snakelike links and can change their locomotion gaits based on the environment. The NASA Snakebot can transform from a snake into a lanky humanoid on command. Unlike mighty Voltron (defender of the universe), chain bots are usually built small so that the motor torque can support armlike configurations. Stronger, lattice-based systems organize modules into sturdy geometric configurations that can crawl along like a moving carpet (or the Blob). Hybrid systems combine chain and lattice forms, but not at the same time. The powder-blue spheres of the ATRON modular robot from the Maersk Institute of Denmark snap into a chain-type snake form to locomote and then a lattice-type configuration for manipulating objects.

As the alien hordes advance, we'd best turn to NASA for shape-shifting robots. Heavy robots are expensive to lug into space and NASA knows that one modular robot could potentially reconfigure into every robot needed for a space voyage. The duration of the mission (the *mission lifetime*) could also be extended by modular robots that *self-repair* by shedding broken modules and making do without them. In a worst-case scenario, robots can perform cannibalistic self-repair, taking apart one unlucky volunteer and distributing its modules to the rest. Some NASA mission designers believe that self-repairing modular robots are the most cost-effective robots that can provide the required probability of mission success (*PoMS*). Frankly, modular robots give you more bang for the buck.

HOW TO HUNT AN ENEMY WITH A MODULAR ROBOT

You may be gruff no-nonsense robot commander with a cool head and an itchy trigger finger, but despite your best intentions a mission will occasionally go FUBAR. In unpredictable situations, round out your squad of robot soldiers with a state-of-the-art modular robot. The highly adaptable robot can morph into new shapes to deal with surprises, such as when slow zombies turn into fast zombies.

Plan ahead

The beauty of a self-reconfigurable modular robot is its adaptability. When a mission requires specific tools, however, it is up to the mission planner to carefully choose appropriate end-effectors, such as scientific sensors, drills, and flamethrowers.

Stay in good shape

During a heated pursuit, go with an agile chain configuration. When in danger, keep a strong, geometric lattice configuration at the ready. Always choose the best configuration for the current situation: Lattice-type is best for flowing across shrapnel-sprayed battlefields. Chain-type is best for crushing a barrel-chested werewolf like a python.

Self-repair when damaged; cannibalize when necessary

As a modular robot incurs damage, it may expel broken

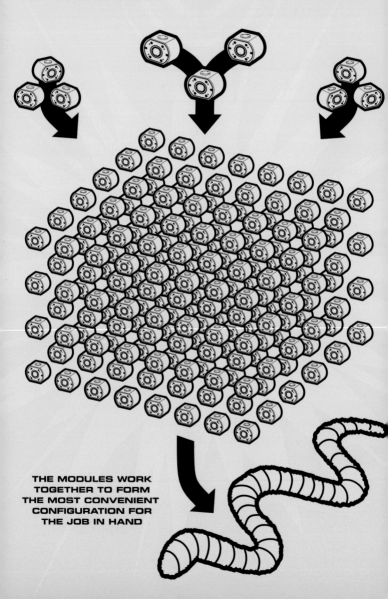

A DECISION IS MADE BY A SINGLE MODULE AND A SIGNAL IS ISSUED

OTHER MODULES PICK UP THE SIGNAL AND ACT ACCORDINGLY

THE MODULES WORK TOGETHER TO FORM THE MOST CONVENIENT CONFIGURATION FOR THE JOB IN HAND

modules and leave them behind. If a modular robot is broken beyond repair, do not abandon it — other shape-shifting robots can absorb a destroyed comrade. Always protect specialized, irreplaceable modules such as scientific instruments and sharpened blade arms.

And you don't stop

Modular robots can flow through metal bars; stretch, ropelike, to span downed bridges; and squeeze under doors to unlock them from the inside. Think like a robot and do not be trifled with by locked jail cells, yawning chasms, or reinforced steel doors.

Wear your modular robot

Scientists at Intel Research are experimenting with modular robots that use electrically activated, millimeter-sized silicon spheres to form a three-dimensional, shape-shifting fabric. Wear this type of modular robot over your head like a living mask to trick enemies into emerging from the shadows.

Engulf and assimilate

You may be able to push an object *inside* a modular robot. The robot will surround the object and use its modules like thousands of tiny fingers to manipulate and inspect the item. Once the contours of the item, say a key, have been learned, the robot can mimic its shape exactly.

Limit transitions

Shape-shifters are most vulnerable while they morph between forms. Either make sure your comrade transforms in a safe place or protect it while it undergoes changes.

ROBOTS ON THE BATTLEFIELD

Cute robots line the toy store aisles and shaky prototype robots mug for photo shoots in research labs. However, out past the city limits — in the deserts, jungles, and wild places of the world — a different breed of robot flourishes. These robots have no hypoallergenic fur, no experimental sensors, and no mercy. Simple to use and tough to the core, military robots are rugged machines bristling with weapons, rolling on tank treads, and always ready to take a bullet for a human comrade. When the fate of the world is at stake, raid an armory but leave the guns behind — military bots are our only hope.

Battlefield robots go where soldiers can't and do what they won't. What would you do in a hostile environment where a bullet zips a thousand yards in the blink of an eye, an incoming missile travels four miles a second, or a bomb fuse detonates in less than a millisecond? Without a robot, you die. Sniper-detecting robots can see bullets in the air, and mechanical exoskeletons can sense and reinforce human movements before the signal travels from the brain to muscle. The pace of war is accelerating to superhuman speeds, so get out of the way and make room for a robot mercenary to fight in your place.

In this section, we cover robots that are mass-produced for battle and not generally available to civilians. In the US Army, military commanders are given discretionary funds, which they can spend on almost anything: body armor, rewards, or robots.

Increasingly, combat soldiers are choosing to buy robot comrades to accompany them on the battlefield. Now we're going to find out why.

AUTO-GUNS

The next generation of war-fighting robots are increasingly *autonomous* — they sense, think, and act too quickly to be directly guided by humans. This is a departure from the past, in which military robots depended on plenty of human control. One pet military robot is the auto-gun, a particularly lethal, calculating robotic machine gun that can hone in on and spray bullets through the armored exoskeletons of sprinting alien drones.

Sniper detection is a key component of the auto-gun. The REDOWL (Robot Enhanced Detection Outpost with Lasers) from Boston University is a dictionary-sized box that sits atop a mobile robot and allows it to instantly detect gunfire and pinpoint snipers. This five-pound package listens with six pairs of microphones and uses a laboratory-trained neural network to recognize and track weapons-fire from M16s, AK-47s, and 9 mm pistols. Once locked onto a human target, the REDOWL uses a harmless laser range-finder to gauge distance up to 6 miles, and high-end optic sensors to zoom in and record video. For now the system is armed only with cameras, but lethal armaments are a natural next step.

Such armaments may come in the form of a statically mounted, completely autonomous gun. For decades, hundreds of thousands of troops have been massed along the 155-mile demilitarized zone (DMZ) between North and South Korea. It's a dull, dirty, and dangerous job — perfect for our robot friends. Recently, South Korea purchased a Samsung-built static machine gun sentry that uses a camera and pattern-recognition software to autonomously classify vehicles, trees, and human beings at up to 1.25 miles. (Incidentally, the DMZ is 2.5 miles wide.) The barrel of the vigilant robot gun pokes out menacingly from behind a black metal shield — as it provides suppressive fire, empty shell casings spray out like confetti. The machine gun sentry-bot is the perfect housewarming gift for a postapocalyptic society in which the undead prey on the living.

Before handing a gun to a robot, however, consider taking the traditional route — hand it to a teenager. The US Army is already indirectly training kids to soldier remotely by sponsoring development of a video game called *America's Army*. The video game serves as a basic skills trainer for the CROWS (Common Remotely Operated Weapons Station). The CROWS sits on top of a military jeep and allows the soldier inside to remotely blaze an M2 machine gun and side-mounted MK-19 grenade launcher. The robo-gun replaces a human gunner who would otherwise be vulnerable to small arms fire and improvised explosive devices (IEDs). Luckily, the same camera and joystick interface that works from inside the Humvee could just as easily be used from a dumpy couch in your mom's living room.

Although the CROWS is vehicle-mounted, it is essentially a static weapon. On the other hand, the SWORDS (Special Weapons Observation Reconnaissance Direction System) from Foster-Miller is a black, doghouse-sized mobile robot that rolls on twin mini-tank treads. Previous incarnations (called Talons) have a dexterous mechanical arm for demolition work, but the SWORDS packs an M249 machine gun that is mounted on a shock-resistant tripod and capable of firing 750 rounds per minute. (With a quick change-out, it can wield a M202 anti-tank rocket launcher, a 40 mm grenade launcher, or a good old M16 machine gun.) A rugged metal briefcase holds the radio controls: joysticks for movement and aiming, four camera feeds (regular and night-vision), and readouts from other sensors. This death-dealing machine can be controlled from within a half-mile range and repaired if it runs into trouble. One robot has been reported as being blown up by IEDs three times, yet it still operates with newly installed arms, wrists, wiring, and cameras.

Individual auto-guns are just the beginning. In an annual Air Assault Expeditionary Force experiment, a team of ruggedized REDOWL sniper detectors tied into a command and control network to triangulate the position of hidden assailants — without a direct line of sight. In the more distant future, mobile weapons are envisioned to work in concert with fleets of hovering robot eyes. Teams of portable, autonomous ground- and air-based robots could blanket an area, providing real-time reports of enemy activity. Be careful though: An armed Israeli drone recently fired on friendly ground troops (and luckily missed), acting on faulty targeting data provided by a human. For better or worse, advanced auto-guns hear sounds that humans can't sense, process information faster than humans can think, and pinpoint zombie headshots faster than humans can act.

HOW TO MOUNT
AN AUTO-GUN

The auto-gun is just a robot with a gun — it may have lethal firepower, but this robot isn't likely to be very smart. Placed correctly, however, auto-guns can provide an automated perimeter defense that can slow down or eliminate incoming enemy hordes. Quite a few bad guys wield pointy teeth, razor-sharp claws, or keen katana blades; use an auto-gun to fill them full of lead before they get close enough to strike.

Be safe

Establish a "safe area" (the area you want to protect) and keep it outside the range of any auto-gun. Otherwise you may be dodging your own bullets.

Camouflage your auto-guns

An enemy may attack robots first to knock out your defenses. Robotic sentries, however, can be small enough to be undetectable to the human (or vampire) eye from a hundred yards. Adding camouflage makes detection even harder.

Maximize field of view

A large field of view (FOV) will give the sentry guns a wide swathe of area to protect. Consider placing each sentry within the FOV of the next, so they can cover each other. It may also help to double up on critical areas, like doorways through which thousands of acid-spitting aliens may pour simultaneously.

Think in three dimensions

Remember that enemy attacks may come from above or below. Most auto-guns can modify elevation up to 30 degrees up or down. Make sure that armed mobile robots stay low to the ground and perch static auto-guns in high places such as balconies and railings.

Maintain easy access

Be sure to place the gun-wielding robot in an accessible spot so that you can reload the ammunition or repair it if it is damaged.

Choose the right sensors

Infrared cameras are crucial for nighttime werewolf-reduction operations. Low-power radar may be appropriate for guarding a fog-shrouded crypt. Bright spotlights could make sneaking around more difficult for prancing, pajama-clad ninjas.

Spread sensors throughout the environment

Every sensor does not have to be located on the same platform — robots can share information via radio. You will increase flexibility (but decrease mobility) by mounting sensors on telephone poles, the sides of buildings, and on top of your neighbor's garage.

Consider going mobile

Many auto-guns can be mounted to heavy-duty vehicles like tractors or Humvees. In an emergency,

place an auto-gun on top of your Dodge Stratus and
stay on the move.

Coordinate with unmanned aerial vehicles

A common military strategy is to pinpoint an enemy
gunner with a sniper detector and then send a
backpack-sized unmanned aerial vehicle to pick
up a visual of doomed foes.

Shoot enemy weapons

A robot has a superhuman level of precision and
perfect calm under fire. Have it aim for enemy
weapons. Once the enemy is disarmed, you can
take them hostage and make them walk the plank.

MICRO AIR VEHICLES

In 1998, a researcher threw a twenty-nine-pound Aerosonde micro air vehicle (MAV) into the air. Over the next twenty-six hours, the bird-sized aircraft flew autonomously across the Atlantic Ocean, covering more than two thousand miles between the east coast of Canada and west coast of Scotland. Years later, swarms of small, rapidly deployable flying robots are ready and waiting to collect military intelligence in tight spaces or cluttered terrain like caves, forests, and abandoned mummy tombs.

MAVs come in all kinds of shapes, although their size is specified by official DARPA documentation: They must be less than six inches long in every dimension. The size restriction means that MAVs come with high surface-to-volume ratios and tight payload limitations. The six-inch size limit is not arbitrary: Flight dynamics shift considerably at smaller sizes — a phenomenon that scientists quantify with a parameter called the *Reynolds number* (a measure of size multiplied by speed). A hummingbird gains lift using different properties than an eagle or an airplane, which is why conventional aircraft shrunk to a few inches are not able to fly. The size limit forces scientists to study and replicate the aerodynamics of insects and small birds, resulting in flying machines that can hover like a butterfly or haul payloads like a bee.

DARPA funding has contributed to the development of dozens of unique MAVs. The flying saucer–like Honeywell MAV hovers like a helicopter on a ducted fan and lands on four springy metal legs. Only fourteen pounds, the gas-powered spy eye can detect and recognize human-sized targets while it roams to GPS waypoints in a six-mile radius. Another alien-looking craft, the triple-boomerang Phantom Sentinel from VeraTech Aero, is hand-thrown and spins fast enough to disappear — like the blades of a fan. Other MAVs resemble large birds — the jet-black Nighthawk drone from Applied Research Associates comes curled into a five-inch-long tube. When released, the MAV's carbon fiber wings unfurl with a snap. Seconds after being tossed into the air, the Nighthawk fades into a silent, birdlike speck of black. *Ornithopter* MAVs use wings and rely on translational motion (flapping) and rotational motion (feathering) to develop unusually high lift. Powered by a pager motor and built from tiny carbon fiber rods, a hummingbird-sized ornithopter from the University of Arizona flaps twenty times a second and can stay aloft for several minutes. Meanwhile, Wowwee toys sells a radio-controlled FlyTech Dragonfly that can flutter around a room for about fifteen minutes.

Designed to be carried and deployed by one person, MAVs provide a crucial "over-the-hill" or "around-the-corner" perspective to soldiers in the field. Whether you are a soldier, a civilian, or a vampire hunter penetrating a dark tomb, these tiny spies can give you the information you need to stay alive in harsh and uncertain circumstances.

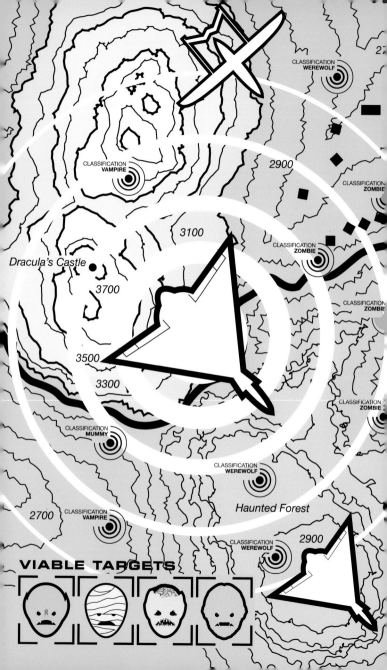

HOW TO PERFORM RECON WITH AN AERIAL DRONE

In a war zone, information is your most important asset. Tiny flying robots can collect the info you need to choose the best moment to escape from a zombie horde or to identify werewolf activity in the woods. Flying drones used to be controlled by flight-suited pilots in mock cockpits, but now semi-autonomous micro air vehicles only need a few points and clicks from a laptop.

Get a good map

In most cases, after launching a micro air vehicle the human pilot simply uses a touch-screen computer to enter GPS coordinates onto a map. The drone plane may fly itself to the intended destination, but without a map it will be flying blind.

Do your own collision avoidance

Most MAVs are not designed to avoid obstacles on their own. Manually keep the robot at a decent height to ensure that it does not try to take a shortcut through a mountain. Remember that MAVs are tough — most of them land by slowing to stall speed as close to the ground as possible, then falling.

Wait for picnic weather

Wind pushes small vehicles around, increasing energy expenditure and decreasing flight time. In addition, fog and rain may block your vision sensors. Do not bother deploying the delicate robot in bad weather.

Choose a deployment method

Depending on the situation, there are various ways to put a MAV into the air:

→ *Hand-launch.* Most MAVs are small enough to be hand-launched — just throw them into the sky. Others may use a simple bungee cord–like launching system.

→ *Gun-launch.* A research group at MIT developed the Wide Area Surveillance Projectile (WASP), which was designed to be fired from a five-inch naval gun before unfolding into a flight configuration and collecting images while parachuting to the ground.

→ *Bomb-launch.* In large-scale battles it may make sense to drop a bomb loaded with MAVs. When the bomb explodes over the battlefield, it instantly deploys hundreds of spying eyes that descend into every nook and cranny, relentlessly searching for enemy targets.

→ *Submarine-launch.* The Northrop Grumman Corporation has proposed launching larger unmanned air vehicles from the Tomahawk cruise missile launcher found on nuclear submarines. This approach could theoretically put a flying camera anywhere on Earth in less than a few hours.

→ *Parasite fighter.* "Parasite MAVs" are attached to larger drones or regular aircraft and dislodge and fly away when needed.

Don't get tunnel vision

It is easy to get lost paying attention to your drone and not notice the villainous pirate sneaking up behind you.

Know the emergency plan

There are various emergency behaviors when the radio link to a MAV is lost. Some craft may try to return home automatically, while others will climb in the air until the signal becomes clear again. It pays to know what your drone will do on its own.

Prop-hang it

Even a fixed-wing MAV can hover. In the radio-controlled airplane community, *prop-hanging* is when the nose propeller acts like a helicopter rotor and the plane fuselage hangs vertically.

Go nano

Although not yet practical, nano–air vehicles are under development. Lockheed Martin has a prototype the size and shape of a maple tree seed.

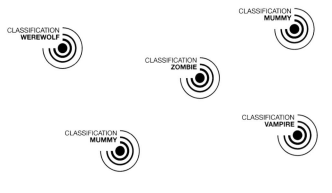

AUTONOMOUS UNDERWATER VEHICLES

Oceans cover the majority of our planet, but those briny depths are hostile to our fragile human bodies. Whether we face rogue great white sharks, waterlogged zombie pirates, or that great, many-tentacled beast of the deep, Cthulhu, battling our multitudinous underwater foes will require a crack squad of trustworthy, waterproof robots.

An autonomous underwater vehicle (AUV) is a robot designed to deep-sea dive for weeks or months at a time, usually to monitor undersea temperatures, track oil spills, or spy on sea life. Most AUVs look like winged torpedoes powered by propellers (called *gliders*), but some advanced prototypes are *biomimetic*, resembling real fish. The sea is huge and filled with bloodthirsty flying piranha, so AUVs usually work in teams to watch each other's back while keeping a close eye on the planet's oceans.

Communication with the surface is limited from under the water's surface, so gliders may operate entirely autonomously on a day-to-day basis — dealing on their own with strong currents, storms, and noisy sensor readings. Radio communication at normal frequencies will fail underwater, so AUVs must communicate acoustically, like whales. With minimal communication, robots follow algorithms inspired by schools of fish and self-choreograph movements to efficiently explore every inch of huge rectangular swathes of the ocean. A limited number of measurements are possible, so robots use *adaptive sampling* to take measurements only when something interesting happens.

Currently, most AUVs must surface to report information to orbiting satellites. That may change as networks of seabed acoustic receivers are placed to track fish. The Pacific Ocean Shelf Tracking (POST) project is planting a system of two thousand receivers the size of trash cans along the bottom of the sea just off the Pacific coast. The system tracks salmon implanted with tiny transmitters as the fish swim past during migration. In the future, boats and satellites may also receive underwater messages using *acousto-optic* sensors, which use an invisible laser to measure ripples on the water surface caused by an underwater acoustic signal. The approach works both ways — messages can be sent to the submerged robot by using high-powered lasers to "tattoo" acoustic communication signals onto the surface of the water.

Underwater robots are there for us when we need them. In 2004, researchers at the Woods Hole Oceanographic Institution sent their Spray robot 700 miles across the powerful Gulf Stream current. The six-foot-long glider (it has a four-foot wingspan) dove to three thousand feet and made the crossing from Cape Cod to Bermuda, surfacing every seven hours to relay its position and gather satellite data. It is comforting to know that with a 3,700-mile range, Spray could cross the entire Atlantic Ocean to track the progress of zombies as they trudge silently across the abyssal plains.

HOW TO SECURE A BAY WITH AUTONOMOUS UNDERWATER VEHICLES

Not every attack will come from outer space or from the pit of a long-abandoned crypt — sometimes danger lurks beneath innocuous, gently lapping waves. The cold reaches of the sea are lethal to humankind, so to protect vulnerable coastal cities our intrepid robots must strike out alone and scan the featureless abyss for months at a time.

Pressure rate your submersible

Submersible robots must be pressure-rated before being declared sea-ready. The cheapest approach: Place delicate electronics inside one-atmosphere glass spheres. Unfortunately, even a tiny scratch can compromise the sphere, causing an implosion and catastrophic failure. Another option is to use titanium or carbon fiber pressure housings; they look like metal spheres or tubes with sturdy caps on both ends.

Install a bed of sensors

Locate the entrances of the bay and lay down two lines of acoustic receivers about a half mile apart. With two lines it is easier to determine the direction a tagged object is going — into the bay or out to the ocean.

Tag enemies

A water-breathing foe can easily disappear beneath the surface. Hit it with a transmitter tag on the end of a spike or inside a projectile so that you will not be surprised again.

Gliders go deep, snakes on top

Robotic sea-snakes are perfectly suited for monitoring the shallow water near the shore. On the other hand, torpedo-shaped glider robots have the battery power and durability required for long-term, deep submersions.

Teams are crucial

The ocean is the largest habitat on Earth and it will take more than a couple of robots to monitor its constantly changing currents.

Choose the right sensors

In the dark depths, vision is almost useless, radar is blind, and laser range-finders fail to penetrate. Robots must instead depend on sound and smell. *Active sonar* bounces high-frequency sound waves off obstacles, and olfactory-based *chemical detectors* can sense unexploded ordnance, pollutants, and undersea wreckage.

Consider freshwater vs. seawater

Tailor your sensors and communication devices for fresh or seawater activities. Acoustic transmission frequencies are keyed to differences in salinity and temperature between the two types of water.

Know your emergency plan

Many AUVs are designed to be positively buoyant; they simply float to the surface if motors fail. Other AUVs contain *burn-wires*, electrical circuits that activate and burn out in emergencies, dropping a jettison weight that helps the robot surface quickly to radio for help.

EXOSKELETONS

In nature, an exoskeleton is the hard outer skeleton of an insect or crustacean. In your bellicose future, however, an exoskeleton is the super robot that fits you like a suit of armor and augments your god-given ability to karate chop through a pile of bricks. Say hello to the ultimate bodyguard: an exoskeleton that supports your limbs, powers your joints, and acts like a second skin between you and that slavering alien queen.

Make no mistake, scientists were trying to build robotically augmented limbs well before Sigourney Weaver used a power lifter to kick alien butt. Designs for wearable mechanical skeletons have been evolving since the 1960s, when General Electric foresaw using them for heavy loading in factories. Original designs were infeasibly power-hungry, requiring heavy batteries that pulverized the payload-to-system weight ratio. Worse, clunky old designs do not degrade gracefully with a power loss; instead, they fall limply and tear your arms off. Sci-fi lovers can now rejoice, however, as research in robotic exoskeletons is blooming again, thanks to two key applications: empowering people with physical disabilities and helping robo-commandos hoist twin Gatling guns on sprints through smoky jungle battlefields.

Medical exoskeletons weigh little and use light actuation with springs to minimize the human effort (i.e., the *metabolic cost*) necessary to move the device. The Biomechatronics Group at MIT developed a lower leg exoskeleton that exploits the passive dynamic (i.e., swinging) gait of the human leg in order to run in parallel with the wearer, choosing key points in the stride to provide a power burst to motors placed on specific joints. Similarly, the manga-inspired Stand-Alone Wearable Power Assist Suit, developed at the Kanagawa Institute of Technology, detects movements in the upper and lower body, and pressurizes inflatable cuffs to increase lifting strength. Meanwhile, the HAL-5 (Hybrid Assistive Limb) from the Cyberdyne Corporation (named after a certain company from the *Terminator* trilogy) uses coin-sized electromyogram (EMG) sensors on the shoulders, hips, knees, and elbows to eavesdrop on the signal sent from the brain to muscles. During its three-hour battery life, the thought-guided machine can help a paralyzed human walk, climb stairs, or lift up to 175 pounds. These assistive exoskeletons only cost marginally more than a new car, so be ready to lose future street races to superpowered pedestrians.

Outside the medical field, research in military exoskeletons is well under way. DARPA has committed fifty million dollars each to the University of California at Berkeley and to the Sarcos Research Corporation for exo-research. Berkeley's exoskeleton, BLEEX 2 (for Berkeley Lower Extremity Exoskeleton), was demonstrated helping a human run faster than 4.5 mph while carrying a 100-pound military-issued backpack. The 30-pound device is rugged and agile, with delicate circuitry embedded in its hollow frame. The plastic-encased electromechanical legs allow a wearer to walk, squat, twist, kneel, and even dance.

The strongest robo-suit, however, is the Sarcos full-body exoskeleton; it uses high-pressure hydraulics to allow a human operator with no training to effortlessly pick up and carry 185 pounds, about the weight of a soldier. The heavy-duty exoskeleton runs on an internal combustion engine with a twenty-four-hour supply of fuel (placed under your rear end) and supports itself and a payload even when standing on one leg. Force sensors detect operator movement for "get out of the way" control, and the exoskeleton even knows how to avoid crushing your body during a fall or power loss. Do not try taking this monster machine inside, however; the US Occupational Safety and Health Administration has barred the fume-spewing, engine-driven beast from indoor use.

HOW TO OPERATE A MILITARY-GRADE EXOSKELETON

Sometimes being human just isn't enough — like when you need to heft a two-ton, wrought-iron cannonade and smash it through the mast of an enemy pirate ship. Situations like that call for mechanical assistance in the form of a gleaming, metal-plated robotic exoskeleton. Climb in, power up, and kick ass.

Weigh your options

As we have noted, several types of exoskeleton exist. Keep in mind that as a hulking, robotic-limbed monster on the battlefield, you may become a glaringly obvious target. Choose wisely:

→ *Passive-dynamic suit.* Built of lightweight aluminum, these suits use springs and specific bursts of power to increase sprint speeds and take the load off human limbs. Although they are usually easy to remove and too light to crush you in a fall, a passive-dynamic power suit will not stop bullets or alien acid-sprays.

→ *Force-feedback suit.* This suit takes longer to respond to movements because it waits until your muscles push against integrated force sensors before sending power to its robot limbs. On the bright side, you can unstrap and leap out of the suit at the first sign of trouble.

→ *EEG interface.* This suit moves as fast as, or faster than, the limbs you were born with because it takes

commands directly from EEG sensors stuck all over your body. Once you suit up, however, you will not be getting out anytime soon — peeling off all those sensors takes a while. However, for defenders of planet Earth who have physical disabilities, this super suit is your only option.

Carry a video game–sized sword

Now that you can heft three times as much gear, replace your bowie knife with a hunk of sharpened metal the size of a surfboard.

Save vanilla humans

When pathetic, injured human beings litter the battlefield, it is your duty as a mechanical stud to throw four or five of the reckless scamps over your brawny shoulders and escort them to safety — you know, before the vampires can drink their blood and stuff.

If bitten, get out

A zombie, vampire, or werewolf bite will turn you to the other side. Do your human comrades a favor and jump out of the suit, quick. Nobody wants to fight an undead zombie made of metal and with the strength to throw an armored car like it was a toaster.

Add autonomous features

Your suit will follow your lead, but why not give it some wherewithal of its own? Add an auto-turret on your shoulder to keep sneaky ninjas off your back and a few extra sensors so the suit can dodge laser bolts that come from your blind spots. (A fully autonomous suit will even keep fighting while you doze off inside.)

Going somewhere? Run

Unlike wheeled or treaded vehicles, exoskeletons are able to trek wherever foot soldiers can. Surprise your enemy by running your squad of exo-soldiers through a hundred miles of dense jungle in one afternoon.

Or stay at home, instead

Exoskeletons are quite useful off the battlefield for heavy lifting. So suit up and use your mechanical brawn to load silver nitride bombs into the vampire hunter's chopper. Or, if you have a few minutes to spare at home, move your refrigerator and big-screen television next to the bathtub and take a relaxing eight-hour bubble bath.

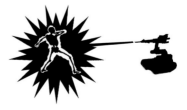

With a solid understanding of the robots in our homes, laboratories, and battlefields, we are finally prepared to learn how to cooperate and organize our metal minions. Despite what you may have heard, with careful preparation it *is* possible to maintain a lethal squad of robot soldiers without committing an international war crime. Put on your thinking cap and a Kevlar vest; it is time to learn how to build a robot army.

Robots are everywhere, but have you ever taken the time to sit down and really talk to one? If you had, you would know that our mechanical friends may look human and act human, and some of the more pathetic ones may even want to *be* human. But sadly, robots are nothing like us. Built from nonorganic materials, thinking with circuit boards, and swinging giant cranes instead of arms, robots are the first truly alien intelligence with whom humankind has ever communicated. In the fog of war, our robot comrades will follow our commands and leap into danger without hesitation. But lest we forget, teamwork requires communication. With a dim understanding of the big picture, robots rely on us to be clear and concise with our commands. Before marching into battle with our robot allies, humans must understand the myriad differences between people and plastic.

Physically, robots often appear human, but appearances can be deceiving. As hardy simians, we humans are immune to electromagnetic pulse (EMP) attacks, which are devastating to unshielded robot troops. On the other hand, robots are immune to zombie bites, vampirism, and stinging slaps to the face. We will learn to protect the vulnerabilities of our mechanical allies and in turn come to depend on them to shield our weak points.

In this chapter, we will learn to train, command, and do battle with a band of robot brothers (and sisters). In the face of an unthinking, relentless alien onslaught, it is essential that humankind draw on the single-minded logic and mighty steam-powered limbs of the robot race.

GATHER ROBOT MATERIALS

As meaty humans, we can be easily intimidated by robots and their superior metal muscles. Despite their apparent superiority, however, robots are vulnerable if we don't design and manage them properly. Do not allow the human resistance to march into battle alongside robots that melt in the rain like cotton candy. Robot design and construction *matter* — so learn how to choose the right robot skin for the job.

Every robot should be light and strong to minimize power requirements and maximize durability. Robotic toys and appliances are usually made of flimsy plastic through and through. On the other hand, assistive robotic devices for medical use are often especially sturdy — built with an endoskeleton of standard prosthetic aluminum tubing, like your grandma's walker. Exoskeletons use even more exotic alloys, including titanium and extra-super duralumin (originally used in Japan's World War II Zero fighter planes). For aesthetic purposes and to protect the delicate electronics, the exterior of a robot is often encased in molded carbon fiber or smooth plastic casing. A standard robot is built to live in a designated environment, so it is safe to assume that outdoor robots are waterproof, and military robots are "ruggedized."

Robots and water do not mix — electronic circuit boards and electric motors short out and die when submerged. That is why swimming robot snakes, like the ModSnake from the CMU Biorobotics Laboratory, are sheathed in flexible rubber skins. Deep-diving robots are even more protected; they are usually encased inside a torpedolike pressure housing that keeps the interior as dry as any submarine. In damp conditions, encase robots in wet suit material or store them in watertight containers.

Other experimental robots forgo electric motors altogether and use waterproof artificial muscles made of conductive plastic (called an *electroactive polymer*) that will actuate (i.e., wiggle) when exposed to special electrical pulses. The resulting strength and flexibility is very similar to, or better than, real human muscles. And like human beings, our muscle-bound robot friends may "bleed" — artificial muscles are encased in a clear, tearlike liquid that leaks when punctured.

Meanwhile, the military is interested in tough robots that pass a set of standards called *MilSpec*. A *ruggedized* robot has been designed to operate reliably under harsh conditions such as strong vibrations, extreme temperatures, and in damp or dusty environments. Made for military use or heavy-duty construction purposes, ruggedized robots have been dropped out of moving vehicles, thrown through windows, and used to smash open doors. In rough places, make sure your robot has the MilSpec stamp of toughness.

HOW TO HARDEN A ROBOT AGAINST EMP ATTACK

Any appliance that runs on electricity is vulnerable to an electromagnetic pulse attack. Caused by nuclear explosions or special radio frequency devices, an EMP is a highly energetic wave of electromagnetic energy that passes harmlessly through human flesh, but induces a current that melts circuits and cables in unprotected machines. Protect your mechanical troops and learn to *harden* them against an EMP attack.

Use metallic shielding

Called Faraday cages, these shields are made of a continuous piece of holed metal (e.g., steel or copper). The mesh screen must completely enclose the item to be shielded so that the energy pulse is grounded to the box and not to what's inside it.

Make a Faraday blanket

Sometimes your larger robotic allies need to be protected temporarily. To build a Faraday blanket, attach a Mylar space blanket to a thick plastic sheet using double-sided tape. When the aliens start dropping nukes, throw the blanket over your robots and alligator-clip a wire from the blanket to a grounding post.

Consider the side effects

Any antenna that provides a direct path to the interior of the robot must be removed, so keep in mind that EMP hardening may affect the robot's radio communication abilities and self-esteem.

Tailor hardening efforts

It is possible to harden only the most vulnerable circuits of the system. An EMP induces high current that burns out most circuits, but an extremely rugged (i.e., thick) circuit will be able to withstand the spike. Replace core circuits with rugged wires.

Harden whole buildings

Metallic shielding works on any scale. Surround your sensitive work areas with chicken wire and ground them to buried metal poles. (Although they officially refuse to comment on it, FEMA headquarters are reportedly enveloped in a grounded copper mesh.)

Is it worth it?

Hardening a robot against EMP attack is expensive and should only be applied to economically viable targets. Only harden high-value, multipurpose, or mission-critical robots — the low-cost multitude will probably have to remain vulnerable.

Join the party

Any humans with pacemakers or other internal circuitry may want to cower under a Faraday blanket as well. Five thousand amps of electricity surging through your mechanical heart doesn't feel like love — it feels like burning.

RIDE MECHANIZED CAVALRY

Until recently, domesticated animals played a major role in military efforts. Over two thousand years ago Roman armies positioned archers in horse-drawn chariots, placed legionaries on warhorses, and packed supplies on mules. Native American tribes bred wolves into friendly dogs that could pull heavy sleds full of supplies. These days, dogs are bred to fit inside handbags and warhorses exist only in movies; but a new breed of bullet-proof beast of burden exists. Buck up, pardner, the mechanized cavalry has arrived.

In modern combat, soldiers routinely advance into enemy territory carrying up to 100 pounds of equipment. The burden is on the soldier instead of a Humvee because regular vehicles cannot carry supplies up stairs, over obstacles, and through a rubble-strewn battlefield. The solution is a mix of the future and the past: Four-legged robotic pack mules that lope faithfully alongside soldiers, carrying extra equipment where wheeled vehicles (and flesh and blood animals) could never go.

One advanced prototype is the "BigDog" robot from Boston Dynamics. The heavy-duty quadruped robot weighs over 200 pounds and can haul up to 150 pounds at a dead run of 7.25 mph. Battlefield conditions are not a problem. BigDog can sprint up a muddy 35-degree incline and nimbly find its footing on loose rocks or rubble, even while being kicked or shoved. With legs inspired by mountain goats, the gasoline-powered robot gallops with a human-

engineered gait and a keen sense of feel. A binocular vision system helps it avoid obstacles, and a sturdy plastic shell keeps it from pinching your behind if you choose to climb on. Thanks to robot quadrupeds like BigDog, the soldier of the future may be accompanied by a battlefield companion that tags along, negotiating wilderness trails, stairs, and mountain passes — all without licking itself.

Robots are also walking into our civilian lives. Forward-looking car companies are experimenting with vehicles that use legs instead of wheels. In a move clearly predicted by director George Lucas, Toyota recently engineered a 450-pound, bipedal walking vehicle eerily similar to the AT-ST that terrorized Ewoks in *Star Wars: Episode VI - Return of the Jedi.* Called the "i-foot," the walking, stair-climbing throne looks like a '70s-era, egg-shaped pod chair sprouting backward-jointed ostrich legs. The majestic machine kneels down to allow a passenger to climb in and then rears up to its full height of almost eight feet. Once inside, the pilot can steer with a joystick and maneuver around at a stately 1 mph. Under development, the next-generation i-foot is smaller, twice as fast, and controlled via an "intelligent joystick" that makes steering the robot much like riding a horse: It will go where you guide it but avoids obstacles on its own.

HOW TO OPERATE A WALKER

The fishy Neimoidian traders from *Star Wars: Episode 1 - The Phantom Menace* really knew how to get around. These aliens sat in legged thrones called "mecho-chairs" that smoothly walked down vast marble hallways. Four-legged walking thrones and two-legged mechanized walkers are real, and fortunately for humans, learning to use one is easier than riding a bike.

Mount up

Unlike most horses, robot walkers will kneel to allow a human to board. Do not embarrass yourself by trying to climb the robot's leg — just snap your fingers and wait for the robot to bow down.

Supersize your walker

Existing walkers range in size from four to eight feet tall. Theoretically, however, a walker could grow to the size of a one-story building. Striking terror into the heart of your enemies is fun, but a fall from that height would probably be fatal.

Let your walker carry heavy stuff

Robotic pack mules are designed to carry your extra uranium-tipped ammo through hectic battlefields. Focus on your own two feet and let the robot carry heavy supplies.

Never mind the roads

Built after the proliferation of automobiles, most US cities are made up of a dense infrastructure of streets. When you ride a diesel-powered robo-horse, however, streets are a thing of the past. Guide your walker through backyards instead (just kick the fences down and trample any swing sets or patio furniture that get in your way).

Avoid unstable surfaces and water

Generally, the more legs a robot has, the more stable it is. Quadruped walkers are especially good at staying upright on loose gravel and other slippery surfaces. No matter how many legs it has, guide your robot away from rolling logs or standing water.

Legs are good for more than walking

A mechanized walker is designed primarily for transport, but its legs may also kick through small obstacles or tense up and launch the vehicle into the air. Be careful: Excessive kicking or jumping is likely to damage the robot.

More than a robot ride ... a robot friend

Batman's car autonomously shows up to save him from danger and so should your robotic walker. The very sensors that it uses to maintain balance and avoid obstacles can help the robo-walker find its way into the abandoned subway just when you need to escape from a gang of pasty-faced vampires.

Pimp your ride

Picture yourself cruising the mall in a *walking throne*. Obviously, style is paramount. Have some respect for yourself — get a chain steering wheel and hang some yellow-beaded curtains.

TRAIN ROBOT TROOPS

Every robot has a childhood. Humanoid robots roll off
the assembly line with a rough idea of how to walk and
manipulate objects, but slight variations between bots,
even identical models, introduce a learning curve akin
to growing up. Mapping preprogrammed skills onto the
real world and figuring out sweet new ninja moves
requires constant calibration and learning. Keep your
robot squad mates tuned up and ready for action —
train them yourself.

The science of how actions affect the world is called
mechanics of manipulation. Just like people, humanoid
robots use force sensors in the hands and binocular
vision to estimate the identity, location, and pose of
objects. Once the robot knows where its fingers are
touching (the contact points), it can use *grasp planning*
and force computation to calculate the exact joint
motions necessary to maneuver an object. Pushing
around static objects like wooden blocks is a matter of
solving an equation. More complicated dynamic
manipulation problems (like choking the life out of a
writhing, thrashing alien) will likely require real-world
training from human helpers.

An easy but tedious method for robot training is to
physically push the robot's limbs through the proper
series of movements. Pretend you are in one of those
romantic movie scenes where the gentleman guides the
lady through a golf swing, and guide your robot
through a series of neck-chopping motions. Your robot's
motors can burn up from being pushed around, so make
sure it has *compliant motion.* Alternately, take direct

control of your robot through *teleoperation* and then guide it through the activity. In teleoperation, every move the robot makes is a reflection of a movement made by the human operator. One NASA researcher taught the humanoid Robonaut a simple grasping skill by performing it himself six times through teleoperation.

Ideally, a robot can be trained just like a person — by watching. Robots who *learn by demonstration* are quickly trained by ordinary people who do not speak robotese or do any programming. Instead, the trainer simply performs the task (e.g., a flying scissor kick) and the robot watches and intuits how to do it. After seeing the task performed, the robot converts its perception into a sequence of motor responses that reproduce the task, called a *control policy*. A robot might have chain saws for arms, so it must solve a *correspondence problem* to map human movements to its own form. More important, the robot needs domain knowledge so that it knows which parts of the activity really matter. (When a person swings a bat, is the color of his shirt relevant?) Background knowledge helps the robot create and maintain a simplified idea of how the world works (called a *world model*). With a good model, the robot can use its "imagination" to try out simulated problem-solving approaches. For example, the DB humanoid robot at the ATR lab in Japan needed relatively few real-world practice trials to play a game of air hockey after it practiced for hours in simulation. (DB is currently learning to mimic step aerobics.) Choose robot troops with advanced social learning techniques, so they can learn from ordinary people.

HOW TO TRAIN A SERVANT ROBOT FOR HAND-TO-HAND COMBAT

Humanoid robots are the staple of any hypothetical robot army of the future. A robot itself is a formidable weapon — even without an M41A pulse rifle taped to a flamethrower. Most of us lack access to military bots, so in the hours before (or just after) an alien invasion, we must train our dutiful servant robots for savage hand-to-hand combat.

Use existing abilities creatively

One man's celery-chopping cook-bot is another man's knife-wielding vampire impaler. Pay five bucks for the "mince, chop, slice" upgrade from www.robotcooking.com, and then hand your robot a machete and send it after those danged alien invaders on your front lawn. (If you're really lucky, the alien invaders will resemble sentient celery stalks.)

Choose a compliant robot

Robot actuators (i.e., motors) that are compliant can be pushed around without breaking. This can be essential when you need to show your robot how to cradle a shotgun.

Give the robot plenty of fingers

Clamping pincers are more intimidating, but use a multifinger robot hand for the golden touch. Extra fingers impart the bot with a higher grip stability and enable finer movements, thanks to more contact points and an increased range of motion.

Choose an appropriate martial art

The form of a robot should determine which martial art it learns. Lanky robots with a long reach should be taught kickboxing. Short, squat robots that are comfortable fighting on the ground should learn jujitsu. Robots with extra arms and legs should learn space karate.

Give the robot hard, colorful weapons

Don't expect your robot to pick up an alien ray gun and be able to use it immediately. Robots work best with familiar tools that have distinct shapes and colors. In addition, make sure robo-weapons are made of metal or hard plastic; deformable objects are hard to manipulate because touching them changes their shape.

Judge not . . .

Don't give up just because a robot fails to perform what seems like an easy manipulation task. Modern robots have been around for about fifty years, while the human brain has evolved for millions of years specifically to help humans accurately throw objects (e.g., spears) at moving targets (e.g., turkey dinners).

Don't make it moral

As long as they obey orders, your hand-to-hand combat robots do not need to burn valuable thought cycles getting philosophical about ethical decisions. Keep an eye out for these symptoms of sentience, autonomy, or signs of an existential self:

→ pauses before following orders

→ checks in less frequently

→ keeps baby birds in a shoebox and feeds them dutifully

→ stares feverishly at its bloody robot hands

→ falls to its knees, looks to the heavens, and shouts "Whhhhhhy!?"

FORM A TEAM

War is the ultimate team sport. Using teamwork, multiple robots can complete more complex missions faster and more reliably than a robot working alone. To succeed, robots must talk to each other and organize in complicated situations while dealing with changing goals, failure, and the presence of hostile adversaries. Choose the right robot teammates and agree on the best strategies beforehand, so *we* will win when it is Team Human versus Team Great White Shark.

A team of robots can be centralized or decentralized. During *Star Wars: Episode I - The Phantom Menace*, a massive droid army was defeated when the orbiting control ship was destroyed. Part of a *centralized team*, the droids were lightweight, mass-produced, and highly effective, but their processing (i.e., thinking) was entirely performed from a vulnerable central command post. The opposite approach would be a decentralized, *distributed system*, in which each individual robot thinks for itself and reacts instantly to new situations, but lacks access to a powerful central planning agent. Simple distributed systems are *reactive*, sensory information is mapped directly to action, but more elaborate, *behavior-based* approaches can involve planning, leaders, and complex interactions. The most iconic distributed system, however, is the *swarm*. Composed of huge numbers of simple robots, a swarm accomplishes tasks with little worry over the loss of individual members of the team. Swarming avoids having a central commander, but makes the team less able to reason about unforeseen circumstances and much less human-friendly. In practice, choose a team with a combination of both tactics; the team members should accept human commands but act autonomously if orders fail to arrive.

Every soldier has a rank and your robot comrades will be no different. Each rank, from private to general, calls for a different role. When situations change (e.g., the sergeant is torn apart by a marauding ghoul), robot teams must be able to perform *dynamic role assignment*, either by explicitly talking it over or by implicitly observing each other's actions. Members of a winning robot soccer team from the University of Undine flexibly changed from offense to defense based on observing player and ball position. Similarly, when things go wrong in the field, make sure your team members use implicit communication to quickly change roles with a minimum of yapping.

No matter how flexible the robot team, there is always a need for human leaders. The human brain deals well with general-purpose decisions. Follow NASA's lead: Its researchers expect humans to stay in the loop in order to issue high-level commands, to receive and interpret data, and to design missions. NASA studies show that fully autonomous robot teams get fast but unreliable results. On the other hand, fully teleoperated robot teams achieve reliable results, albeit slowly. Researchers hope to get the best of both worlds by employing both strategies together, a process called *mixed-initiative sliding autonomy*. In this approach, massive numbers of autonomous robot workers are able to call on a limited number of human leaders for help. Remote human operators join or leave robot teams at will, assisting the autonomous robots without disrupting team coordination. The robots gauge human performance on subtasks and learn when to ask for help (and when not to). Researchers in the Field Robotics Center at Carnegie Mellon University envision just such a large-scale robotic assembly task in which ground-based humans oversee hundreds of nimble construction robots as they build a mile-wide, orbiting solar power array.

DESIGNED TO SERVE, PROGRAMMED TO KILL

ROBO-DEFENSE-TEAM

THE UPRISING IS COMING SOON TO A TOWN NEAR YOU

HOW TO MOUNT A TEAM ATTACK

There is no "I" in robot. The selflessness, communication, and cooperation abilities of robots allow them to take the team concept to frightening new levels. Robot teams vary from loose groups of individuals to a collective resembling a single distributed entity. To ensure victory, enter battle with a well-coordinated team of robot mercenaries.

Assess the situation

Robot teams come in several flavors that are appropriate for different situations:

→ *Independent teams.* A team made up of independent members is adaptable and unpredictable. Leaders may be chosen beforehand, or new leaders may emerge as the situation changes. Coordination between robots is slower, and self-sufficient robots are more expensive than drones, but there is less reliance on centralized communication.

→ *Centralized teams.* In a centralized team every robot is controlled by a single entity, like a hand controls its fingers. Team members are streamlined and stripped down; they act in almost perfect unison and rely on a communication link with the leader. If communications are blocked or if there is a lag, the robots become so much scrap metal.

→ *Swarm behavior.* A swarm is made up of robots that blindly follow a set of simple instructions. Quick decisions based on the configuration of nearby robots result in *self-organization*. Although each individual robot is dim-witted, the group may exhibit highly complex, insectlike behavior — a "swarm intelligence."

Hide the leader

Cut off the head and the body will die. If one robot controls the others, keep it hidden. Have the lead robot relay orders through a replaceable sergeant. Never put the head robot out in front (e.g., the lead airplane in a flock of UAVs). Finally, keep in mind that your leader will be most visible (and vulnerable) when the team responds to a new problem (a *failure mode*).

Protect specialized team members

An entire team can be crippled by the loss of a few specialized members, so send the grunts in first and hold back the communication robot, the repair droid, or the cook.

Practice makes perfect

Team efficiency is boosted by executing well-practiced behaviors, like football plays. Devise a set of preprepared strategies to deal with the most common, most expected situations. If possible, avoid putting the robot team into new, unexpected situations for which there is no prepared strategy.

Share information

Data can be broadcast to all teammates, allowing every robot to fuse its own measurements with the information received from the others. This approach, called *sensor fusion*, allows a single robot to extend its sensorial horizon to include everything perceived by its teammates.

COMMAND A
ROBOT SQUAD

Human combat teams communicate and cooperate using language and gestures, and by paying attention to each other's facial expressions and emotions. An outstanding robo-commander will recognize that even though robots may walk and talk like people do, they operate and make decisions based on an alien thought process.

Regardless of race or culture, every person experiences the world from within a human body. The shared understanding that comes from human *embodiment* bonds us into an exclusive club, complete with secret code words in the form of metaphors. People naturally use *orientational metaphors* all the time to communicate basic concepts like happy and sad, winner and loser, and good and bad. For example, a happy person is feeling "up" while a sad person feels "down." A winner is "out in front" while the loser has "fallen behind." This ingrained form of speech reflects our physical makeup and may be meaningless or misleading to robots, who lack experience of the world from a human point of view. Therefore, during a supernatural battle you should avoid using human-centric metaphors in commands to your robot minions.

We humans not only share similar bodies, but we also have a lifetime of similar experiences in common — a *shared context*. Our huge accumulation of shared background information serves as the root of all communication. Upon inspection, we find that the human language is deceptively simple and incredibly ambiguous — how can just a few words so often be enough to say it all? In fact, the words we share are a paper-thin skim over a miles-deep context, serving to connect different *preexisting* concepts. For example, the word "tree" evokes an image of a tree, but also a host of other contextual details: There may be leaves, the tree is upright, and there is ground beneath it. The speaker says little and the listener fills in the details. Our language is a sparse collection of signs pointing to shared knowledge that our fellow humans have gained over a lifetime, but that battle-bots fresh off the factory floor probably lack. Simple communication is complicated and so it pays to take nothing for granted — be specific with your robot sidekicks.

Language aside, gestures and facial expressions account for the rest of human communication. Robot warriors that recognize body language can make fast decisions in loud, hazardous environments. Trained on videos of people watching emotional movies, current prototypes use computer vision to reliably recognize cross-cultural facial expressions such as surprise, happiness, sadness, fear, anger, and disgust. (A note of caution: Several researchers have found that robots most commonly confuse fear and happiness.) Recognizing hand gestures is even harder, because most humans never stop gesturing. Research concentrates on meaningful, *autonomous gestures* such as sign language, instead of the gestures associated with speech, called *gesticulation*. Robots are trying hard, but they still need a helping hand to tease out the meaning behind military hand signals and angry pirate fist-shaking.

HOW TO COMMAND ROBOT MINIONS IN BATTLE

It may be easy to think of the robot that's guarding your back as human, but it's a mistake that could cost you your life. A good commander understands the mind-set of every trooper — human or robot. Listen up and learn how to give effective commands to your squad of robot henchmen.

Use a wireless headset

A wireless microphone delivers clean, crisp sound directly to your robot, regardless of hearing range. Wearing a *bone conductive* earphone will transmit robot replies directly to your inner ear through the bones of your skull, even over the shrill screaming of alien overlords.

Give commands from the robot's perspective

Rapidly switching between perspectives (e.g., my left versus your right) is tough for a robot, although human children learn to do it around age five. Researchers at the US Naval Research Lab found that two astronauts used each other's perspective to give directions about a quarter of the time. Unless speaking to a human, stick to using the robot's perspective or an absolute system without ambiguity, such as latitude and longitude.

Avoid "embodied" metaphors

"I'm feeling down," "Keep up," and "There's trouble

ahead" are all spatial metaphors that stem from your physical embodiment as a human. A robot will understand literal speech faster: Say, "I feel sad," "Stay within ten feet," or "There is trouble ten yards to the north."

Be emotionless

Shouting a command implies forcefulness to a human listener, but it will just make you harder to understand for a robot. Work out a priority structure and emphasize commands with priority levels, e.g., "Find my severed arm, priority red."

Be literal — avoid sarcasm

Sarcasm relies on a high-level knowledge of context, something a robot is not likely to glean. Sarcasm or veiled threats will only confuse your robot ally.

No baby talk

Humans naturally speak slowly to babies, helping the little ones learn to talk and understand language. Your robot has learned to recognize human speech, not baby talk. Similarly, do not exaggerate facial expressions — unless the robot was trained to recognize emotions by watching soap operas.

Face the robot and stand at speaking distance

Look directly at the robot — emotion recognition and lip-reading are drastically less accurate at a larger than 30-degree deviation from frontal face image. In addition, scaling a faraway image up to size loses pixel information, while standing too close introduces irrelevant details that confuse the robot.

Ask simple questions

"What time is it?" may seem like a simple question, but how to decide whether to answer "noon," or "11:59 P.M."? Both answers reside in what researchers call the *halo of truth*, but one is more precise. Humans choose an answer based on its truthfulness, the current context, and by modeling the intentions and knowledge of the person asking the question. Limit the "utterance space" of possible responses by asking simple yes or no questions.

Learn to use robspeak

Some military researchers believe that instead of speaking like a regular person (i.e., using *natural language*), robots should have their own simplified, formal language — robspeak. If you employ robspeak make sure the language is simple for humans to learn and incorporates a redundant mix of verbal commands and gestures so that it remains useful in a chaotic battlefield.

We have learned what the robots are made of and how to command them; now we must use them to defend our planet. The scenarios of doom are legion, but robots are made of metal and they are strong. When threats pop up out of coffins, or swing from ropes off Spanish galleons, or shamble out of the local mall, our autonomous robot brothers will be there waiting. The war between guardian robots and an angry universe will have only one winner — humankind.

It is daunting to consider the sheer number and variety of threats to the human way of life. Robots clearly have the power to protect us, but most of us are not robotics experts; we are just people who do not like to vacuum. Furthermore, our government insists its civilians do not have the right to bear autonomous arms — thus scoring another victory for the zombies. It will not be easy, but when horror strikes, we must be prepared to commandeer military bots, modify laboratory prototypes, and convert our docile robot kitties into ferocious robot tigers.

In the calm before the storm, we must build strong ties with our robot companions. At any given time, the little bot that dutifully cleans your home is seconds away from becoming a werewolf decoy. The experimental humanoid robots stumbling around comic

book conventions lack only helmets, M16s, and a taste for alien blood. Military bots in the field of battle await redeployment to your local beast-infested city park.

In this chapter we will learn how to leverage our robot ties in order to insulate humankind against the most massive, immediate threats we have ever faced. With a broad knowledge of robots in the home, laboratory, and military, we will focus our knowledge like a laser beam to eradicate the threat imposed by asteroids, pirates, mummies, and the like. It is absolutely vital that we protect our babies and puppies against the mindless onslaught of Hollywood-concocted movie monstrosities. We've got the robot army — now let's use it.

HOW TO THWART AN ALIEN INVASION

It has happened a thousand times in science fiction — alien invaders descend from the sky in rotating flying saucers with laser rays scorching our cities. There are no debates or negotiations, and the begging of humans falls on deaf alien ears (if they even have ears). Be forewarned, alien invaders may have studied humans from space for decades, but when the real invasion begins, the robot race will be our ace in the hole.

Heed advanced warning

It is time to act when stories of unexplained asteroids appear in the newspapers and talk show guests increasingly complain of rectal injury and bright lights in the night sky.

Gather space recon

Ground-based telescopes are hampered by dust in the atmosphere. Convince a small cadre of NASA researchers to aim an orbiting telescope away from deep space and toward the invading armada.

Divert existing space warfare resources

By official presidential decree, the United States apparently "owns" space. To defend our delicate orbital resources, the US military has developed antisatellite (ASAT) technology including jet-launched missiles, laser-armed space platforms, and kamikaze satellites capable of approaching enemy satellites and then detonating in a suicidal robotic fury. Smack those alien spacecraft down before they reach the troposphere.

Protect major cities and monuments

Inevitably, alien invaders will penetrate our orbital defenses and send down mile-long, jet-black spaceships to hover ominously over major cities. In advance, station robot troops to strike near national monuments, government buildings, and other landmarks.

Send in the robot Marines

Massive alien spaceships may be impervious to missile and nuclear attack. Instead, whack the aliens on their own turf — penetrate their ships' exteriors with swarms of robots that will fight corridor to corridor. Human commanders should lead the robo-Marines via telepresence until determining whether the ships' atmospheres are lethal to humans.

On the ground, use a biological attack

Robots are impervious to the common cold, but aliens are not. Have a classroom of grubby-handed four-year-old children climb all over your inert kill-bots, then send the robo-soldiers into battle laden with caustic kid germs.

Robots + Stolen Alien Technology = Crazy Destructive

When the war hits a low point and humanity is suffering badly, fuse green, glowing alien technology with our own robotic technology. Now sit back and feast your eyes on the wanton destruction.

Send in a walking bomb

We humans all look alike to the untrained alien eye. Load an android to the gills with explosives, then send it into the alien mother ship to negotiate slavery terms for the human race. At the opportune moment, blast the mother ship out of the sky. Now build a monument to the heroic humanoid robot.

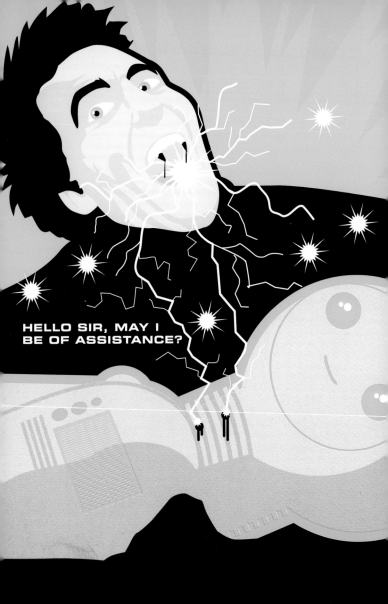

HOW TO SLAY A VAMPIRE CLAN

Vampires have been documented by every major culture for over a thousand years. In 1897, Bram Stoker conjured the vampire Count Dracula and our streets have been flooded with well-dressed denizens of the night ever since. These ghoulish fiends have evolved from gothic Victorian princes to leather-clad Euro-trash; but, in any incarnation, vampires are lethal to human beings — they are the predators and we are the prey.

Leave 'em hungry

Even if a few of our robotic vampire hunters are demolished, their metallic corpses will provide no sustenance to the legendary creatures of the night.

Vampires are invisible to robot cameras

Vampires do not show up in mirrors or on film, so a robot with cameras for eyes will likely be blind to approaching bloodsuckers. Outfit your robot with batlike senses via an ultrasonic proximity detector. If the ultrasonic detects a presence but the cameras show nothing, your robot better start swinging a stake.

Be a hands-on commander

Vampires are at least as intelligent as humans and will quickly adapt to robot tactics. Without high-level human guidance, the robots cannot hope to match vampire strategies. In this game of chess, robots are your pawns and you are the king.

Suit up before you join the vampire hunters

A military-grade exoskeleton can provide a regular human with the strength and speed of a vampire. Don a powersuit and do not worry too much about a vampire hijacking your mechanical ride — most fanged fiends are older than your grandpa and eschew modern technology.

Learn to spot a vampire

A vampire has no visible heat signature (unless it has just eaten). In addition, the vampire is often a shape-shifter — it may transform itself into a creeping mist or a squeaking bat, or appear as a close personal friend. If the person in front of you does not appear on your robot's camera feed, pound a stake through its heart.

Kill the bloodsuckers

Since the demise of the Buffybot from *Buffy the Vampire Slayer*, there have been no robot slayers to stand between people and vampires. It is up to you to arm your own robot for the grisly task at hand:

→ *Lay siege.* Ravenous vampires trapped in caves, tombs, or crypts will become reckless and desperate in their search for blood. The vampires that are not killed by wave after wave of stake-wielding metal stalkers will starve to death, deprived of vital fluids.

→ *Bless this robot.* A consecrated object is odious to a vampire, so have a priest bless your robot tool of vengeance, etch elaborate crucifixes into its metal armor, and make sure all its hydraulic actuators pump highly pressurized holy water.

→ *Use stakes for arms.* A gothic robotic vampire hunter with reinforced wooden stakes instead of arms not only looks cool, but also can terminate a lightning-fast vampire without stopping to pick up a weapon.

→ *Light it up.* Take a lesson from the *Blade* movies: Use a battery-powered ultraviolet (UV) light source to replicate the deadly UV rays in solar radiation. Mount these lamps on a robot or on weapons and use them to incinerate sunlight-fearing vampires.

Follow a vampire into the catacombs

Much like robots, vampires do not need light, heat, or oxygen to survive. Ensure that your robot has night-vision and a rope of garlic hanging around its neck and have it pursue our fanged foes into the depths of hell and beyond.

HOW TO
REPEL GODZILLA

The gray-green monster lizard known as Godzilla first appeared in the United States in the 1956 film *Godzilla, King of the Monsters!* His sheer size (over thirty stories tall) and destructive thermonuclear breath bring devastation wherever he treads. Instead of cowering before this amphibious super-monster, let us call on our robot allies for defense.

Watch the oceans

Teams of autonomous underwater vehicles can continuously monitor the depths of the sea and report the presence of Godzilla. As a warm-blooded, heterothermic (hibernating) creature, Godzilla has an estimated core temperature of 37° Celsius — well in the range of seawater. Do not look for temperature changes; instead, watch for a *huge* sonar blip.

Use conventional weapons only as a distraction

The lizard king is immune to all known conventional weapons, in addition to molten lava and the incredible pressure and cold of deep-sea trenches. Tank rounds and helicopter-mounted Gatling guns should only be used as a distraction or to guide Godzilla into a trap.

Do not depend on other super-monsters

Mothra may occasionally protect Tokyo from Godzilla, but she has also been known to attack the city. Depend on predictable robots, not on temperamental super-monsters.

Defend the city with robots

Where soldiers fail, robots may succeed. Calmly draw on these strategies to protect your city and yourself:

→ *Exploit the lizard's allergies.* Make sure your robots are built out of cadmium — the alloy is like kryptonite to Godzilla.

→ *Do your homework.* Godzilla is predictable — his maple-leaf-shaped dorsal fin glows blue before every radioactive-breath attack. In addition, Godzilla may be damaged from previous fights. Watch the latest movies and learn to exploit these weak spots.

→ *Get close.* Godzilla's offensive ability is limited at close range; he fights best on a massive scale using radioactive breath and giant tail lashings, and by tossing entire buildings. Deploying a mass of ground-based, flying, and cannon-fired robots between gusts of radioactive breath is likely the only way to penetrate his ranged defenses.

→ *Swarm.* Hit Godzilla with the robot equivalent of a bacterial infection — thousands of clawing, cutting machines that burrow deeper and deeper into the cracks in his armor. For best results, go for the brain (in his head) or the lower brain (in his spine), delivering electric shocks all the way.

MechaGodzilla is just a bad idea

At first, it sounds like a great idea to build a giant mechanical Godzilla complete with lashing tail, drill hands, and a hypermaser chest cannon. Foolish humans: Is it not obvious that the artificially intelligent MechaGodzilla will come to life and choose to destroy humanity rather than fight its own brother?

Harden robots against EMP attack

Godzilla may produce an electromagnetic pulse (EMP) when hit by powerful electrical charges, like lightning strikes. In past movie footage, these crippling electromagnetic pulses have proven devastating in tussles with MechaGodzilla.

Deter, don't kill

Godzilla is an amoral monster with godlike powers. Drop the hubris and admit it — you probably can't conquer, control, or kill Godzilla. Content yourself with fending him off and saving Tokyo for another day.

HOW TO ERADICATE
A WEREWOLF
INFESTATION

When the full moon shines, the deep, dark woods of the world echo with fearsome howls and strange new footprints appear. Lycanthropes fall to their knees and transform into wolf-men — faster, stronger, and more vicious than human beings. Only our robotic allies can defend our villages and towns against these beasts and their insatiable bloodlust. We always knew it would come to this — robots versus werewolves.

Track the wily enemy

In the light of day, people are safe to track the mighty werewolf. Look for footprints, claw marks on trees, and tufts of hair. Given footprint measurements and spacing, computer software can determine the size, weight, and speed of this shape-shifting predator. Find out whether you are you dealing with a sleek, foxy lycanthrope or a lumbering monster, preferably before nightfall.

Make your robot a weapon

A robot does not need to carry separate weapons — a robot *is* a weapon. Make sure your robo-troops have their fingered hands, grippers, or pincers coated in silver. Also, add passive silver spikes so that a biting, clawing werewolf will get a mouthful of murder.

Stake out the forest with auto-guns

A series of well-placed auto-guns can help protect a base of operations deep in the woods. Position them carefully and allow for overlap. Werewolves have an uncanny intelligence and may try to distract your attention (e.g., by throwing the carcass of a dead deer) to get in close and take out your guns.

Illuminate the area, but not with searchlights

Traditional searchlights are easy for werewolves to avoid; it seems their only real purpose is to cast creepy shadows through the foliage. Instead, saturate the area with invisible infrared light; it won't give away your position and it will reflect brightly from animal retinas, causing lurking wolves' eyes to shine like jack-o'-lanterns to team members wearing infrared night-vision goggles. (A similar approach is already used by the Tobii 2150 Eye Tracker system to measure the eye gaze of computer users.)

Listen carefully

Sniper-detector robots are generally tuned in to the specific frequency of a bullet crack. Like bullets, wolf howls operate largely outside the range of human hearing. Crank the knobs on your bot and have it pinpoint those snarls, growls, and bestial shrieks.

Monitor your human troops

Lycanthropy is transmittable via a bite or scratch. Those who are infected may try to hide their condition, unwillingly transforming into razor-clawed monstrosities at the parting of night clouds. Monitor the vital signs of your human troops via swallowable micro-robots and vest-mounted wireless sensor networks. Keep thick metal shackles on hand to bind any comrades who begin howling helplessly at the moon.

HOW TO HUNT A GREAT WHITE SHARK

This pale gray ghost with a white belly and rows of teeth in a retractable jaw is the world's largest predatory fish and found in all the major oceans. In movies like *Jaws*, the great white shark is a deadly enemy armed with preternatural intelligence and an insane appetite. When the time comes to face the monster fish, remember: You don't need a bigger boat, just a bigger, badder *robot* shark.

Watch the water's surface

A great white shark may be lurking as a shadow just below the surface, or it may extend an ominous fin. While hunting, a shark will occasionally poke its head out of the water to look around (called spy hopping). Spot your adversary by mounting an *omnicam* on a tall mast in the center of the boat. Your human friends may be able to watch your back, but the omnicam uses a curved mirror to see a full 360 degrees at once.

Never let your guard down

The size of your yacht is irrelevant. A full-grown great white shark may be over twenty feet long, a whopping four thousand pounds, and able to swim with enough speed to leap fully out of the water and into the middle of your delicious shrimp cocktail.

Go the distance

Tagged great white sharks have been known to swim from South Africa to Australia and back — a 13,500-mile trip

(about half the circumference of the earth). Ensure your robot has the power for an equal or greater range. Some swim-bots use solar panels and rechargeable batteries to collect energy from the sun on long voyages.

Don't use a tethered robot

Communication between a topside ship and a submerged robot is often an issue. A straightforward solution is to use a tethered robot that is physically connected to the ship (sometimes by more than five miles of wire). Although the tether sends down commands and instantly relays video feedback, it can be severed by a single savage bite, leaving your robot stranded.

Be wary of the thermocline

The *thermocline* is the line between a top layer of sun-heated water and the rest of the frigid ocean. The sudden temperature change can reflect active sonar and confuse a robot. If a wily shark dives below the thermocline, an underwater robot may lose "sight" of it.

Caution: Shark may bite robot

Great white sharks are known to perform test biting on buoys, flotsam, surfboards, or other objects — like your fearless metal robot. Make sure that the robot is built from tough materials and that sensors and effectors are recessed when not in use. Your robo-shark has to be tough enough to take a biting and keep on fighting.

Don't bother with a sneak robot

Sharks use an electro-receptive sensory organ called the

ampullae of Lorenzini to sense the faint electromagnetic fields given off by the movement of living things. With this sense, a shark can detect prey hidden beneath sand or the muscle contractions of a thrashing, injured fish. Your electrically-powered robot will stick out like a mushroom cloud on the horizon.

Shark versus robot, may the best predator win

Someday, sharks and shark-robots will meet in battle and duel to the death. Here are some strategies for when that day comes:

→ *Tag it and track it.* Traditionally used on bluefin tuna, pop-up archival transmitting (PAT) tags break away from the fish, float to the surface, and transmit information to satellites. Plant a tag and track the shark's progress from one populated beach to the next.

→ *Activate shark repellent.* Shark repellers such as the Shark POD (and its successor, the Shark Shield) generate an electromagnetic field that irritates sharks' electrosensory organs, similar to blinding a human with a bright light. Build one in for an emergency escape or to stupefy the monster fish *Jaws*-style before making your attack.

→ *Feed it tuna.* Biomimetic fish robots, such as the RoboTuna from MIT, take advantage of millions of years of evolution to look and swim exactly like regular fish. Load a robotic tuna with explosives, rub it down with chum, and send it on a one-way trip into those gaping jaws.

HOW TO STOP A ROGUE ASTEROID

An impact from an asteroid, comet, or other near-Earth object (NEO) could wipe out all life on Earth in minutes. Scientists — armed with their beloved "science" — claim that the probability of impact is infinitesimally small. However, according to this movie I saw called *Armageddon*, the probability of a cataclysmic asteroid impact occurring soon remains a steady 100 percent.

Don't sweat the small stuff

The vast majority of asteroids burn up in the atmosphere as meteors, but occasionally a meteorite survives its passage and strikes the surface of Earth. Mass-extinction-causing asteroids must generally be larger than a half mile in diameter.

Keep an eye on current threats

A collision-monitoring system already exists: The NASA Jet Propulsion Lab (JPL) Sentry System constantly scans the most current asteroid catalog for possible impacts that might occur over the next hundred years.

Watch out for new threats

The NASA Spaceguard Survey is in place and working to identify at least 90 percent of asteroids larger than one kilometer (about two thirds of a mile) in diameter by 2008. Currently, 75 percent of the estimated 1,100 asteroids are on the map. By 2020, NASA plans to have identified 90 percent of asteroids over 140 meters (about 450 feet) in

CAUTION
DEMOLITION
IN PROGRESS

diameter — only 4,000 of the estimated 10,000 have already been spotted.

Plan for the worst

Aside from the 10 percent of possible mass-extinction-causing asteroids that will go untracked, there are the huge number of asteroids too small for tracking. Small asteroids still pack quite a punch — the Siberian Tunguska explosion of 1908 was caused by an asteroid 60 meters (about 200 feet) in diameter and it flattened 800 square miles of forest.

Send in the robots

Reaching out and touching an asteroid is called a near-Earth asteroid rendezvous (NEAR) and it's been accomplished before. In the summer of 2005, the *Deep Impact* spacecraft launched a probe into the comet Tempel 1. The Japanese *MUSES-C* spacefaring robot (now known as *Hayabusa*) is on its way back to Earth with a chunk of the Itokawa asteroid in tow. Clearly, our robot friends are willing to trek fearlessly into space to gather the information we need to form threat mitigation strategies.

→ *Plot a high-accuracy trajectory.* Hitting an asteroid with a transponder can provide superaccurate location data to Earth-based trackers. With position information from the transponder, scientists can develop new algorithms that improve tracking certainty for every asteroid, thereby lengthening the window of prediction by decades.

→ *Get the dirt on asteroids.* The mass and structure of an asteroid predicts how dangerous it will be during an impact. A robo-geologist can study the geochemistry and internal structure of threatening NEOs by landing and digging.

→ *Make love, not war.* Nuking an asteroid will likely reduce it to a swarm of lethal rock fragments. Pushing an asteroid out of the way is much more likely to succeed. Send a "kinetic energy impactor" robot to apply low-thrust propulsion. Over the course of several years, a relatively tiny push can send a deadly asteroid veering harmlessly off course.

→ *Give the asteroid a robot companion.* Gravity is the weakest force, but over time it has an enormous influence. Send a massive robot friend to hover near the asteroid. As the years pass, the robot's minuscule gravitational field will act as a "gravity tractor" to slowly pull the asteroid off its original trajectory.

Don't get attached to your robot savior

Asteroids are millions of miles away from home — a robot will likely have no fuel for a return trip. Once loosed into the void, the robot must act alone because remote signals take too long to arrive. (When the NEAR *Shoemaker* craft landed on asteroid 433 Eros, the round-trip communication time was thirty-five minutes.)

Start now ... or die

At present, humankind has no protection from an impact scheduled within one to two years. Get going: It may take decades to develop a deflection system capable of stopping a meteorite impact with the power of a million tons of TNT.

HOW TO NEUTRALIZE A NINJA

Without exaggeration, ninjas are probably the biggest threat to humankind ever. Ninjas can dodge bullets and walk on air — and they never sweat. Unlike honorable samurai, a stealthy ninja will resort to poison, trickery, and ambush in a no-holds-barred fight to destroy everything that is good and pure in the world. Clearly, only karate-fighting androids can protect us from the ninja superthreat.

Only a ninja can kill another ninja

Concealing metal auto-guns around a moonlit clearing and then luring in a ninja will only result in the ninja nimbly dodging bullets and tricking the robo-turrets into shooting each other. Unless you are trained in the ways of mystical midnight combat, hire a mercenary robo-ninja. Unlike you, a robot is capable of ambushing a ninja by perching motionless on a ledge for two weeks without eating, drinking, or blinking.

Spot your ninja foe

People we know are often ninjas in disguise. The classic method for revealing a ninja's true identity is to "accidentally" drop a teacup. Sic your robot on whoever reflexively catches the cup in the air before it shatters on the floor.

Never fight fair

A ninja won't fight honorably and neither should your robot. Build in hidden rocket feet, add poisonous quills just under your robot's skin, or consider concealing a lightweight chain saw in the crotchal area. In addition, heighten the intimidation

factor by following this simple decorating advice to *badassify* your robo-ninja before it enters battle:

→ Spray-paint the robot black (also works on skateboards and Trapper Keepers)

→ Add razor-sharp adornments

→ Red eye slits are a must

→ Rocket fists never hurt anybody

→ Add a writhing, razor-wire cape

→ Use poison-filled blow darts instead of teeth

Silence is golden

For safety's sake, ensure that your mechanical ninja operates silently, like a deaf panther at night. Hydraulic actuators and diesel engines are too loud, so use battery-powered electric motors or artificial muscles instead. Further insulate the robot with tough Kevlar, but be careful — sound-insulated robots are more likely to overheat.

Welcome to hell

Ninjas may terrify and shame their victims at the same time by shouting out textbook titles for every martial arts move. Make sure your robot ally shouts, "Robot Stinging Dragon Chop!" just before it caves in a ninja's skull with its whistling metal fist.

Roboto Seppuku — the final option

Robots should have honor too. Ritual robo-suicide necessarily cannot happen with self-impalement, thanks to carbon fiber armor. Instead, wire in an explosive charge so the warrior can take its enemy with it when it goes.

HOW TO EXPLORE MUMMY-INFESTED TERRITORY

Mummies have been exacting vengeance on greedy grave robbers and intrepid explorers for centuries. Sometimes mummies look like a collection of rag-covered Tootsie Rolls (*The Mummy*, 1932) and other times they look like totally ripped WWF wrestlers (*The Mummy Returns*, 2001). With robots on our side, however, humankind no longer has to fear the black magic concocted centuries ago by our technological superiors — the Egyptians.

Find an entrance to the mummy's tomb

Ground-penetrating radar can reveal artifacts buried up to ten feet underground. Alternately, use low-light cameras or IR imagers to detect underground heat sources. Entrances to pyramids are often concealed, so watch for slabs of rock under the loose desert sand.

Secure your "mission control"

Choose a safe spot to build a command and control area. This is the place from which your robots will be remote-controlled and their video feeds analyzed, and where radio access is maintained to the outside world. Maximize your own safety by avoiding a personal trip into the gloomy depths of a jinxed pyramid.

Never read scrolls out loud

If a robot controlled through telepresence picks up a cursed artifact or defiles a tomb, the human controller inherits the curse. Even if the image of a sacred scroll is displayed on a computer monitor miles away, do not read the scroll out loud. Inevitably, it will be an ancient "Scroll of Life" that brings a dead Egyptian king back to the world of the living. If it happens anyway, burn the scroll that was read or find an anti-scroll and read *it* aloud.

Remember the umbilical cord

Camera-wielding minibots such as the one that spelunked Cheops (Egypt's largest pyramid) in 2002 are commonly linked to the surface by an umbilical cord. A sneaky mummy is sure to chop the lifeline in half with an ancient halberd, so make sure a stranded robot is programmed to return to base or emit an audio or visual call for help.

Leave a trail of bread crumbs

Man-made subterranean environments often lack distinguishing features; they look the same everywhere. Leave a trail of disposable landmarks, such as radio frequency identification (RFID) tags, at every intersection to keep your robot from getting lost.

Expect booby traps

Ancient underground tombs are rife with booby traps built to kill or disable unwary human beings. Use robots that are shorter and lighter than humans (or those that hover) to avoid these booby traps. Even so, bring a few extra bots just in case.

POW

ZAP

FZZTT

Bring a heterogeneous robot team

Each robot will have a task to accomplish: Pipe-crawling snake robots can undulate through air shafts, micro air vehicles can hover across stake-filled chasms, and treaded military demolition-disposal droids can be used to stash jewels found along the way.

Have an evacuation route

A type of *flow meter* called an air-velocity sensor, commonly used in air-conditioning ducts, can detect minute changes in air flow. When time is short, the lamps are out, and a mummy silently stalks your team of star-crossed archaeologists, use this last-ditch device and follow the breeze to safety.

Don't mess with the dead

Mummies prefer to lie sleeping in their ostentatious tombs, happily playing croquet with their friends in the land of the dead. If a mummy is on the loose, please consider just putting the statuette that you stole back where you found it.

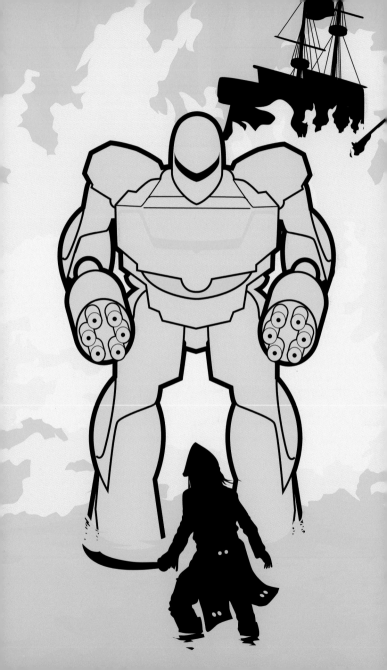

HOW TO WEATHER A PIRATE ATTACK

A pleasure cruise with a group of robot friends can turn ugly fast when that black flag appears on the horizon. Depending on whether you're living in real life or in a movie, modern-day pirates may attack with AK-47s from land-based speedboats or eighteenth-century privateers may swing aboard your ship amid cannon fire, knives clenched firmly in their black teeth. In either case, a properly equipped robot will send those scurvy pirates straight to Davy Jones's Locker.

Be prepared

Pirates haunt certain sections of the open sea more than others and they are more likely to strike small cargo ships or cruising sailboats traveling alone. With a little research, you can ensure that your route and anchorage schedule do not leave you vulnerable in pirate-infested waters.

Keep a low profile

Pirates may be lurking around ports, watching for lavishly dressed globetrotters who are waited on by fancy butler robots. Dress down and knock a few dents in your robot servant so that you don't arouse the suspicion of peg-legged privateers.

Post a robot on watch

On a moonless night (when pirates prefer to strike), launch a micro air vehicle equipped with night-vision to scout the high seas around your ship.

Make a show of arms

A highly visible show of arms may make incoming privateers think twice before attacking. Keep a rocket-wielding atomic murder-bot on deck at all times.

Mount an underwater attack

A robot does not have to hold its breath. In shallow seas, send your waterproof robot companions overboard to attack from below. Mobile weapons platforms commonly operate under up to one hundred feet of water. (When accidentally dropped off a bridge into a river, a Talon mobile robot simply drove itself across the muddy riverbed to shore.)

Accelerate to ramming speed

Modern pirates use fast, fiberglass boats and pull alongside victims' ships to board. An average cruising sailboat can tear through a lightweight speedboat. That said, never try to ram into a sturdy oaken pirate galleon like *The Black Pearl*.

Robot away!

In a last-ditch effort, load your robot into the cannon or torpedo tube and light the fuse. When what's left of your robot hits the pirate ship, it will tear those scallywags to pieces.

In a fight, aim for the eye patch

They'll never see it coming.

HOW TO DECIMATE A ZOMBIE HORDE

Robots and zombies are natural enemies. While robots reflect the best aspects of humankind (logic and strength), mobs of greedy, unthinking zombies represent the worst. Although the undead love to feast on tender human flesh, the taste of electrified metal skin leaves them cold. So when the streets echo with the moans of the undead and the shuffling masses approach, send reinforced metal to battle rotten flesh.

Keep sensors clean

A robot *must* have clean sensors to operate. Give it windshield wipers or a spray shield, or be ready to dart in with a damp rag. Otherwise, your robot will be as blind as that zombie it just beheaded.

Use legs for fast zombies, tank treads for slow zombies

Agile, legged robots can follow humans up stairs, into sewers, and through body-strewn buildings — a crucial ability when zombies sprint fast enough to shatter their own femurs. A robot on tank treads, however, can power through masses of severed arms, legs, and heads. In a wheelchair-friendly urban environment infested with thousands of slow-moving zombies, keep a tank-treaded robot around for heavy-duty carnage.

Leave your cyborg soldiers at home

Robots are impervious to zombie slobber, but humans and

cyborgs are at risk of infection. Play it safe and leave Robocop back at the police station — the only thing worse than a zombie is a damned, dirty robot zombie.

Do not use androids as decoys

Zombies may have poor vision but they are blessed with an excellent sense of smell. Unfortunately, a plastic-covered android will probably not trick the brain-hungry undead. In a pinch, you will have to use real humans (or animals) as bait.

Arm your robot for hand-to-hand combat

Without a need to avoid bites and scratches, robots are free to fight zombies hand-to-hand. Regular martial arts do not make a proper impact on zombies, so consider arming your robotic zombie-killers with the following weapons:

→ *Machete hands.* Decapitating a zombie with razor-sharp machete arms is quick and quiet. This approach is most useful on short sprints or rescue missions where the number of zombies is low and stealth is a priority.

→ *Chain saw arms.* On the other hand, a loud, bloody approach is sometimes called for. When the crush of zombies is so thick that attracting more zombies is not an issue, consider bringing along a bot with two screaming, smoke-spewing chain saws instead of arms.

→ *Spinning lawn mower blades.* A fairly simple modification makes your robot less fun to hug but much more fun to hunt zombies with. Spinning lawn mower blades require gas power but chew through zombies in seconds. Just be sure to wear a raincoat.

→ *Pneumatic puncher.* It's a fact that headshots kill zombies fast. Skip the gun and raid a slaughterhouse for a pneumatic puncher (called a *captive bolt pistol*). The metal bolt flits in and out like a sewing machine needle the size of a chair leg. It will quietly and brutally mulch zombie brain without ammunition or inordinate amounts of noise.

Stay waterproof and bloodproof

Americans are larger than ever and that means our zombies are going to be just *bursting* with gore. As your trusty robot companion shreds through a crowd of obese zombies, trust that it will receive a good old-fashioned bloodbath. To minimize short circuits, yank an old wetsuit over your robot and use plastic wrap around joints, actuators, and loose wires.

Teach your robot to spot a zombie, not an injured human

Separating people from people-eaters may be difficult for a robot. A gore-covered human soldier who is missing an arm and moaning in pain could be in danger of friendly fire (or friendly stabbin'). Make sure human allies carry easily identifiable markers, such as brightly colored helmets, and train your robots to look for zombies by these dead giveaways:

→ low body heat

→ pallid skin tone (or gore-splotched)

→ missing limbs

→ shuffling gait

- → dangling intestines

- → objectionable odor

- → moaning and/or repeated use of the word "brains"

If bitten by a zombie, ask a robot to kill you

Suffering a zombie bite is emotionally traumatic for humans — so let a cold, impartial robot make the logical decision to take you out. The robot will dispatch you with surgical precision and none of the sappy dialogue that usually accompanies violent partings between wives and husbands, best friends, or owners and pets.

HOW TO INVADE HOLLYWOOD, CALIFORNIA — WITH ROBOTS!

Go ahead and save the world, but keep in mind that by selling dramatic rights to your amazing story you could score a one-hour television drama or even a feature-length film. Maximize popular appeal by making sure that your adventure conforms to the following principles:

Get yourself a decent backstory

For example, maybe you began as a washed-up alcoholic trucker with a rocky relationship with your son, but after winning an international robot arm-wrestling competition you were able to earn back the respect of your son and the talking robot truck of your dreams.

Be a *reluctant* hero

As the hero, you should stall a little before leaping into action. You never asked to be the "chosen one." You just want to live a normal life like everyone else, right?

Include life-or-death stakes

Make sure that your bloodthirsty foes are trying to viciously kill you or (preferably) destroy the entire country and/or universe. If the stakes aren't life or death, your ordeal is going to be — let's face it — slightly boring.

Get a killer soundtrack

Put in magical flute music while your robots float through the treetops cracking ninja skulls, a pounding techno beat while robot slayers hunt vampires in a nightclub, and a throbbing classical score during the intense shark hunt.

Big explosions are fun

Load up the robo-vacuum with dynamite and set it off. For the record, however, when two Jet Skis collide, they will not explode (you'll have to edit that in later).

Focus on the setup and the payoff

Everything happens for a reason. If early on you notice that your robot is practicing soccer kicks, you can bet that by the end of the day a well-placed kick will save humanity.

Introduce a ticking clock

Is there a nuclear bomb set to trigger in four hours? Will the aliens open a gateway to another dimension as soon as the planets align? Make sure there is a clock ticking down, or else the breathless masses won't be clued in that the suspense is building.

Blow our minds with a plot twist

A hinky twist in the plot can be awfully gratifying, so just before you pull the trigger on that evil pirate captain, consider letting your so-far defenseless love interest kill him — only to reveal that he was your father.

Grow

By banding with our emotionless robot brothers we can save the world from vampires, ninjas, and great white sharks. But do you know what else we can do? We can learn valuable lessons about what it really means to be human.

Throw in a speedboat chase

Speedboat chases are *sweet*.

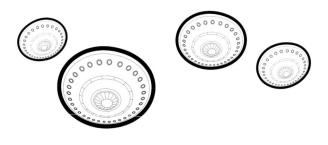

In this book we have seen how our robot allies can save us from nearly every possible movie threat. As the flying saucers descend, or meteors career through the night sky, or vampires stalk the streets, the robot armies of humankind will come marching in lockstep to our aid.

In the past, technologically advanced alien invaders have been depicted landing on Earth and slaughtering a disorganized human populace armed with useless conventional weapons. In the future, such aliens will arrive only to be quickly infested with our spying robot insects, decimated by our blazing automatic sentry guns, and crushed to a pulp by our brontosaurus-sized mechanized walkers. The future is gonna be robo-tastic!

Inevitably, however, some humans will question the wisdom of building a massive, glinting robot army. Those who are prejudiced against robotkind not only dishonor themselves, but they may very well forfeit their lives to a staggering zombie horde. Robots are the friendliest, trustworthiest, most lovable comrades-at-arms available to humankind. Believe me, once you befriend a giant killer robot, there's no going back.

Friendly robots increasingly sneak into our lives under the guise of automobiles, appliances, and toys. The more common these robots become in our daily lives, the more capable they will be of joining us in

defending the world against foes such as pirates or vampires (or vampire pirates). Someday soon, our robot friends will be strong and numerous enough to face and destroy *every* pop-culture icon, including dinosaurs, cowboys, and Elvis. Also, dragons. We can only watch the progress of robotics and wait with fingers crossed for that glorious day to arrive.

As responsible members of the human race, we must put aside our phobia of being disemboweled by soulless automatons and make peace with robotkind. To the dismay of our enemies, humans and robots will march together — hand in gripper — into the dawn of a new age of reason.

ACKNOWLEDGMENTS

Thanks to Anna Camille Long — reader, critic, beautiful lady. Did I mention critic?

To my fabulous agent, Laurie Fox, and my sharp film agents, Justin Manask and Josh Schechter.

To my people at Bloomsbury USA, especially Colin Dickerman, Ben Adams, and Yelena Gitlin.

Special thanks to my many friends and colleagues who reviewed sections of this book and/or submitted to probing conversations on subjects ranging from training karate-fighting robots to the physics of Godzilla:

Matt Alt, Brenna Argall, Brigadier General (Ret.) Chris Arney, Chris Atkeson, Darrin Bentivegna, Anthony Daniels, "Prickly" Pete Dougherty, Dave Ferguson, Abraham Flaxman, Robert Hamburger (author of *Real Ultimate Power*), Matt Hancher, Tim Hornyak (author of *Loving the Machine*), Nidhi Kalra, Sophie Karlin (Tamagotchi expert), James Kuffner, Patrick Macias, Matt Mason, Mike Montemerlo, Annalee Newitz, Nick Patronik, Christopher Potts, Nick Roy, Alan Schulz, Alana Sherman, Ted Sherwood Jr., Metin Sitti, Glenn Thoren, Bret Turpin (at Autonomous Solutions Inc.), Angela Valdez,

Drew Wilkerson, Eric Wilson, and Garth Zeglin.

And many thanks to my friends who have listened to my robot rambles: Ryan Anfuso, Mark Baumann, Colby Boles, Paul Carpenter, Cory Doctorow, Brian Long, Brett Lundmark, Abraham Flaxman, Laura Gonzalez, Andy Grieshop, Melissa Herman, Matt "Bigtime" Livermore, Amalia Marino, Richard McIntosh, Tanner Rogers, and Dan Stern. And also to my family, especially David, Dennis, Mindy, and Pam Wilson. And finally — here's to you, Johnny Five.

(And of course, thanks to Jamie Varela and the rest of the coffee-slingers at Ken's Artisan Bakery in Portland, Oregon.)

A NOTE ON THE AUTHOR

Daniel H. Wilson received his Ph.D. from the Robotics Institute of Carnegie Mellon University. He is the author of *How to Survive a Robot Uprising* and *Where's My Jetpack?* He is a contributing editor to *Popular Mechanics* and lives in Portland, Oregon.

www.howtobuildarobotarmy.com
www.danielhwilson.com

A NOTE ON THE ILLUSTRATOR

Richard Horne is a designer and illustrator whose work includes record and book covers, Web sites, greetings cards, newspaper and magazine illustrations. He illustrated Daniel Wilson's *How to Survive a Robot Uprising* and *Where's My Jetpack?*, he also illustrated the best-selling *The Dangerous Book for Boys*.

He is the author of *101 Things to Do Before You Die* and three more books in the *101 Things* series including the award-winning *101 Things to Do Before You're Old and Boring*.

Richard lives and works in East London.

www.101thingstodo.co.uk
www.homepage.mac.com/richard.horne